Routledge Revivals

Recording in Social Work

Originally published in 1972 *Recording in Social Work* looks at how recording has always been claimed as one of the necessary activities of social workers, whatever form of social work they undertake. The book deals systematically with recording, and the theory and practice recording takes, as well as the research projects and small-scale studies which discuss critically certain aspects of the method. The book offers a review of the history of recording, including a critical discussion of the three early texts on the subject. It surveys the literature on purposes of recording and concludes with an analysis of the main issues surrounding recording. The book assesses the present position of theory and practice in social work recording and suggests both ways in which the subject can be developed and the wider context.

Recording in Social Work

by Noel Timms

Routledge
Taylor & Francis Group

First published in 1972
by Routledge & Kegan Paul Ltd

This edition first published in 2018 by Routledge
2 Park Square, Milton Park, Abingdon, Oxon, OX14 4RN
and by Routledge
711 Third Avenue, New York, NY 10017

Routledge is an imprint of the Taylor & Francis Group, an informa business

Publisher's Note
The publisher has gone to great lengths to ensure the quality of this
reprint but points out that some imperfections in the original copies may
be apparent.

Disclaimer
The publisher has made every effort to trace copyright holders and
welcomes correspondence from those they have been unable to contact.

A Library of Congress record exists under LCCN: 72194409

ISBN 13: 978-1-138-36448-6 (hbk)
ISBN 13: 978-0-429-43133-3 (ebk)

Recording in Social Work

Noel Timms

*Professor of Applied Social Studies,
University of Bradford*

LONDON AND BOSTON
ROUTLEDGE & KEGAN PAUL

First published 1972
by Routledge & Kegan Paul Ltd,
Broadway House, 68-74 Carter Lane,
London EC4V 5EL and
9 Park Street,
Boston, Mass. 02108, U.S.A.
Printed in Great Britain by
Northumberland Press Ltd,
Gateshead
ISBN 0 7100 7288 0 (c)
0 7100 7289 9 (p)

General editor's introduction

The Library of Social Work is designed to meet the needs of students following courses of training for social work. In recent years the number and kinds of training have increased in an unprecedented way. The Library will consist of short texts designed to introduce the student to the main features of each topic of enquiry, to the significant theoretical contributions so far made to its understanding and to some of the outstanding problems. Each volume will suggest ways in which the student might continue his work by further reading.

This book is divided into three main parts. Chapter One makes some historical observations on social work recording, illustrating the broad phases through which the subject has passed—in this, as in other aspects of social work history, we have as yet to be content with rather crude generalizations. This chapter ends with a brief comparative analysis of the three texts so far available on social work recording. As the subject of recording leads into so many other aspects of social work, so the treatment of the subject may serve as a model for the study of other aspects. Comparative analysis of social work texts is long overdue. The second chapter reviews the main objectives usually cited in discussions of recording—service, teaching and research. Existing work on the nature of these objectives is reviewed, and a possibly fruitful direction for future work is indicated. Finally, in a discussion of some critical questions the author draws our attention to recording behaviour, the results of keeping a record and the difficulties in making one. The Appendix, which presents three different modes of recording the same interview, makes a contribution to the study and also suggests an exercise that students might usefully perform on their own work. Since this study largely takes the form of a literature review, the guide to further reading usually in this Library is, literally, taken as read.

The record holds an important place in any of the main methods of social work—casework, groupwork, residential work and community work. Yet, as the author states, we have no contemporary text on the subject. The present work is not intended as a detailed guide to the practical problems of recording, but as an attempt to assess our present ideas and knowledge about recording so that tasks for the future can be more precisely described. Such a critical treatment is important not simply because it is hard to conceive of any evaluated social work without records, but also because within what can be described as 'the problems of recording' we can see in miniature some of the central problems of social work.

'And what in observation is loose and vague
is in information deceptive and treacherous'

Francis Bacon

Contents

CONTENTS

x

Acknowledgments

I would like to express my sincere thanks to Tricia Sharp who worked efficiently and cheerfully as my research assistant during the writing of this book. I am also indebted to John Hart for the case records in the Appendix.

Introduction

The absence of a contemporary British text on social work recording seems neither noted nor mourned. The topic appears to lack both appeal and urgency, and this is somewhat strange. The supposed or possible achievements of social work are often debated, but for the last hundred years or so most social work interventions have had one actual and undeniable result—some kind of record of the business transacted between agency and client. The history of recording in social work is as long as the history of modern social work. Moreover, the student's record and recording have played an important part in social work education since formal training began. The emphasis in evaluation has undoubtedly changed from a concern with good habits in what a student once described as 'methods of personal service and case-paper work' to a close criticism of the recording of the process of an interview: recent British books on student supervision consist largely or almost entirely of such detailed recordings (Heywood, 1964; Kent, 1969). Despite this important change 'records' of some kind have featured in the training of students for a good many years.

Recording is evidently of importance in social work but contemporary textbooks devote little or no space to the systematic discussion of the purpose, methods and use of such recording. Hollis (1964) gives 2 out of 266 pages,

Wilson and Ryland (1949) allocate 10 out of 619 pages on social group work whilst Perlman (1957) is silent on the subject. It is rare to find an author such as Davison (1965) devoting a chapter to the topic. Yet these and other writers clearly accept the social work record as a fact of existence, and Hollis in particular uses the systematic study of actual records to establish and justify an elaborate typology of casework treatment. Recorded material (suitably disguised) is, of course, a marked feature of most social work texts, but little or no attention is given to the problems of recording, let alone to problems raised in any claim to have 'a record' of such complicated phenomena as the interaction of two or more human beings.

It should not be assumed that social work recording has been ignored in other kinds of contemporary writing or at other periods in the history of social work. A literature of social work recording does exist—and this book largely takes the form of a critical bibliography to acquaint students with its dimensions. The last text to be published is by Hamilton (1946) which followed and used the two earlier books by Sheffield (1920) and Bristol (1936). The major part of the literature, however, consists of articles dealing with particular aspects of recording (e.g. diagnostic recording, the use of tape recording). More recently reports of specific pieces of research on recording have started to appear. Aspects of the literature will receive consideration later, but reference to previous writing is made at this point because it shows both the importance accorded to recording in social work over a period of time and also can be used to indicate some reasons for the current neglect of the systematic discussion of the subject.

Earlier writers on records gave the topic considerable importance in social work. Richmond judged that it was 'upon such case history study, in fact, that social casework will have to depend, in large measure, for advancing standards and new discovery' (1917, p. 99). Sheffield noted:

'Memory is deceptive, and can easily persuade a well-intentioned person to think she is doing well by her client as she means to do ... It is not too much to say that a case work agency that keeps poor records is giving ineffective or superficial treatment to its clients' (1920, p. 13). This essential connection between recording and effective practice becomes one of the major assumptions in the literature. Thus, a professional statement in 1949 judged that 'The social record is indispensable in rendering effective service to the patient and in maintaining social casework practice' (American Association of Medical Social Workers). The firmer the assumed bond between recording and effective service, of course, the more difficult it becomes to prise the two elements apart for separate analysis and the easier to subdue any doubts with a definition—such as: un-recorded casework is somehow not casework.

The literature on recording gives ample testimony to the acknowledged importance of the subject, but it also suggests that practitioners often fail to live up to the predominant method adopted by writers to secure adequate or improved recording in the field—namely exhortation. Critical comment on the actual practice of recording forms a continuous feature of writing on the subject. Three quotations from different times will illustrate this as well as indicating the kinds of adverse criticism made. Thus, Richmond in 1917 found some of the crucial steps in the process missing: 'Case records often show a well-made investigation and a plan formulated and carried out, but with no discoverable connection between them. Instead, at the right moment, of shutting his eyes and thinking, the worker seems to have shut his eyes and jumped' (p. 348). The Younghusband Report (1959, paragraph 606) often failed to find any formulation of plans in the social work records of the (then) health and welfare departments of the local authority.

Good social work records are needed in these services. It appears to us that these tend to be poor or non-existent partly owing to pressure of work and lack of clerical help, and partly because their value is not always recognised. We saw a good deal of totally inadequate recording which did not go much beyond names and addresses, as well as some well-kept and informative case papers. Both we and the field investigators frequently noted with regret the lack of an adequate social history or of information on which to base appraisal of a situation or evaluation of progress, or on which a new worker could plan his initial approach to an individual or family. The whole concept of providing a social work service by the most appropriate officer or department breaks down if records do not contain basic data and significant facts. Insufficient information affects the department concerned as well as officers in other services which may be called in. It also makes it impossible to evaluate the service given or to work out, follow through and test the effect of any consistent course of action. We recommend that every effort should be made ... to encourage better case recording ...

Finally, a quotation from Rennison (1962, p. 67) indicates a criticism that moves beyond that of incompleteness or basic inadequacy: she questions, as do several more recent authors, the actual use of records at least in some social work agencies:

Social work records tend to amble along, full of descriptive and evaluative material but so verbose and so lacking in point or structure that reading them is tedious and unrewarding. Frequent repetition in long records suggests that social workers themselves rarely re-read their words, but apparently are satisfied to commit their thoughts to their stenographers and then leave them for posterity.

So far in this introduction we have been concerned with the facts that recording is of crucial importance in social work (an importance that is also stressed in the literature) and that there has been no systematic treatment of the subject since Hamilton (1946). Part of the explanation of this discrepancy can now be seen to reside in the practitioner's marked lack of enthusiasm for the topic. Recording is perhaps one of the best illustrations of the gap that is said to be a feature of many if not most aspects of the relationship between 'theory' and practice. A second explanation can be found in the character of much of the literature, a lack of conceptual clarity and of a critical approach. It is only comparatively recently that serious research has been undertaken. For most of the time the literature has been content to propose for the social work recorder a set of purposes (apparently of a commonsensical kind), to illustrate extensively a small number of key concepts (such as process recording), and to exhort the practitioner to do better. The literature is predominantly of this kind because the subject of recording is neither as simple nor as capable of separate treatment as at first sight appears to be the case. Recording cannot satisfactorily be considered apart from some of the most difficult and central issues in social work, and this, of course, adds to the problems of writing even a short text on the subject. It is not easy or perhaps desirable to separate questions concerning the purposes of recording from difficulties about the purposes of social work. If we raise questions concerning the differences particular theoretical positions might make to the content and style of recording we are involved in precisely these questions asked of social work as a whole.

In this situation it is important to delineate the shape and boundaries of this book. It will be concerned with tracing in outline the history of recording and with surveying the literature in order to describe the various treatments accorded to the subject and to discover the extent and justification of any agreements that can be found. This book will also attempt to present the main problems in the subject. The aim is not to teach directly 'the best ways to record', but by examining past treatment and present problems it is hoped that the student will be helped towards an appreciation of the present state of knowledge in the realm of recording. The focus of past work has been mainly upon social casework. In this book the focus will be widened by considering both other methods of social work and, where appropriate, experience in other occupations.

It is of some importance to appreciate that most if not all of the problems encountered in social work recording are paralleled in a whole range of organizations. From the point of view of the organization serious problems arise in connection with the acquisition of 'good' material and also with its use at the most appropriate time. The introduction to a reader on the subject of recording noted that 'a great deal of the materials that accumulate in organizational files is never referred to, never read, and never acted upon' (Wheeler (ed.), 1969, p. 13). Perhaps this 'failure' takes on a more positive aspect when we begin to consider the record from the point of view not of the recorder but of 'the client'. The book just referred to suggests that a record has five generic characteristics. It is more likely than informal types of communication to attain *authority*; it has *permanence*; it is *transferable*, so that 'We can speak of records as literally having a life of their own'; it is *faceless*, in so far as it can easily become disassociated from the person who wrote it; it can be *combined* in many different ways, often without the knowledge of the person whose life chances it may be helping to determine. If we begin to view recording in social work within the wider context supplied by this kind of comment our discussion is likely to benefit, and it is possible that the problems and challenge of the social work record may contribute to the fruitful exploration of the important set of general problems constituted by 'the record'.

1

Historical observations

It is not easy to reconstruct in any detail the history of recording in social work. A few studies of actual records over varying periods of time have been made, but the object has usually been to trace general changes in methods of work and assumptions rather than to describe in detail changes in the form and style of recording. Thus, Clement Brown (1939) refers to her unpublished study of eighty records compiled between 1924 and 1934. She suggests that this indicates a shift in the social worker's attention from certain kinds of behaviour (e.g. honesty, cleanliness) to personality and a greater emphasis on the account an individual himself gives of his life and situation. Alsager MacIver (1935) makes a brief comparison of the slim records of 1899 and the much stouter volumes of 1935. In the former, 'the consideration and discussion of underlying motives is also absent and one feels that case-work has gained by making a study of these and an attempt to fathom them before deciding on a plan of help'. More recently an impressionistic study (Timms, 1961) of sixty-eight sets of case papers from the Charity Organisation Society covering the period 1887 to 1937 concluded that

> for most of the period caseworkers work on a founda-
> tion of practical theorems; they expect reasonable be-
> haviour and the maintenance of moral standards and

they show faith in the plasticity of human nature. They collect information with varying degrees of care, judge it according to the views of the ordinary practical, moralising citizen and administer with varying degrees of warmth and success routine procedures which have the authority of time and the support of cumulative but unrefined tradition.

These and other studies show that old social work records help us to see broad changes in social work but they provide only indirect illumination of changes in the theory and practice of recording. A satisfactory history of recording—as of all other aspects of social work—is still needed, and in this section we have to rely almost exclusively upon secondary sources. These sources will be used in two ways: to indicate broadly what appear to be the main changes in recording practice and in attitudes towards 'the record', at least so far as the social worker is concerned; and to provide a comparison of the only three texts devoted to the subject of recording in social work (Sheffield, 1920; Bristol, 1936; Hamilton, 1946). These texts are, of course, American, but British work on this subject is extremely sparse and scattered. Between 1912 and 1947, for example, the Journal of the Charity Organisation Society refers hardly at all to the subject.

Some broad changes

Recording in social work seems to have gone through four more or less clearly differentiated phases, though it would be difficult to associate any one phase with a defined period of time. The first phase is perhaps best characterized as that of the register-type record. In using single line entries to record the names of clients and the help given or not given, social agencies were beginning to keep records, but only just, as the following examples will indicate:

Name (Fictitious)	Cash (American currency)	Residence	Remarks
Mary Peters	1.50	City	Sick with cancer.
John Robbins	2.00	City	Broken leg.
Josephine Adams	1.00	City	Partly blind.
Elizabeth Carter	2.00	City	And 3 children.
Margaret Riley	1.50	Ireland	Drunk H. 3 ch. under 8.
James Smith	1.50	City	Sick, wife & destitute child.
William Jones	1.00	City	Large family.
Susan Miller	1.00	City	Widow, etc.
Marie Schmidt	2.00	Germany	Destitute.
Martha Campbell	1.00	Scotland	Aged and destitute.
Julia Williams	1.00	Maryland	Ditto.
Mary Winston	1.00	City	Ditto.
Walter Simpkins		City	Died this month.
James Davis	1.00	Ireland	Injured by a fall from a horse.
Winifred Waters	1.50	City	Lame and has an idiot son.
Annie Flanagan	1.00	Ireland	Widow, 79 in March.
Jessie Bryant	1.00	City	Very aged.
Michael Sampson	1.00	City	Non compos.
Celia Cohen	2.00	Russia	Wife of Joseph. Left her.

(Source: relief agency *c.* 1839 quoted in Sheffield, p. 7.)

Entries of this kind must have been a feature of poor relief agencies for centuries.

The second phase of recording in social work probably began in the second half of the nineteenth century. It was characterized by more detail especially in relation to the client's own statement of his or her problem, the verification of what were seen as certain key facts, and the recording in abbreviated diary form of business transacted with the clients or in connection with their affairs. An early study of case records noted that 'early case-papers show that the office work and enquiries were all done by one person, a paid agent—brief and formal in his reports, much impressed with discovering the character of each applicant' (*Fifty Years Ago*, 1926). The aim of the Charity Organisation Society to bring order and businesslike efficiency into

RELATIONS (Names and Addresses) He ....

....

She ....

....

References ....

....

Date	
12.12.45	Miss B. phones to know if we would visit this woman who is suffering from rheumatoid arthritis, and is bedridden. Her husband and son are out at work and she could manage to pay for the sheets herself, but hers are in a very bad condition and she has no one to get out to see about it. Promised to visit.
13.12.45	Visited but got no reply at all. The key was in the latch. I walked in and called several times but got no reply.
14.12.45	Visited. Knocked hard several times but no reply.
18.12.45	Rang Miss B. to find out if she knew of any special time we could call on Mrs Brown or any way we could get in the house. She said the home help usually went in the mornings but she thought that the key was on a string just inside the front door letter box. She asked us to ring her again if we visited and still found we could not get in, though she thought one of the neighbours could probably help us.
21.12.45	Called and was able to see Mrs Brown. She was in bed and appeared to be completely crippled. She has a home help and a nurse coming in to look after her. She was rather deaf, and conversation was a little difficult. She said she really needed blankets or a warm quilt rather than sheets, but that she would like flannelette sheets as they were so warm. Apparently she is rather heavy on bed clothes because of her complaint. She said she could not afford to pay the entire price but would be willing to pay a little in instalments. Did not take down financial particulars

	as Mrs Brown said the Town Hall had them all, and I did not want to tire her unduly.
6.1.46	Rang Miss B. re outgoings and incomings. She was unable to give us the first names of the family but she gave us a detailed account of their expenses. She thought it would be a good thing if Mrs Brown paid a little towards the blankets.
10.1.46	Called and gave Mrs Brown a quilt, she was terribly grateful for it and said 'it was like coming into a fortune'. She said she thought they could afford to pay a few shillings a week for flannelette sheets which she wants badly and she would like to buy a blanket, but does not want us to see about that until she has discussed it with her husband. She would also like some pillow cases. She would like us to see about the sheets at once as she needs them badly. Arranged to call next week and tell her what we could do.
11.1.46	Called at the Stores to see if they had any flannelette sheets. They had none but expected some in February.
16.1.46	Sanction quilt. Leave to District Nurse who is dealing. (This item is recorded in red.)
	After committee nurse said she would ring us to-morrow morning about what they had done for Mrs Brown and what they planned to do. She would be glad if we would give pillow cases as they have none.
16.1.46	Nurse phoned to say they had given sheets at Christmas and two blankets, no pillow cases. Could we give these and if anything else was needed nurse would phone.
17.1.46	Called and gave Mrs Brown two pillow cases, she was very grateful.

the muddle of voluntary social work is very evident in the attention given to the records that the Council of the Society expected its district offices to keep. *Books and Forms* is the rather ominous title given to a Charity Organisation Paper first published in 1871. A Visiting Form

CONFIDENTIAL

_____ Committee   Form 22.

CHARITY ORGANISATION SOCIETY.

CASE No._____   Date. 12th Dec. 19 45

Surname_____   Floor._____ Church Parish

Cases sent by_____   Address_____   Birthplace._____

Name and address of Present Landlord._____   Time there_____   Religious Denomination_____

Previous Addresses, Landlords, and Time at each {_____   Medical Adviser_____

Assistance asked for _____ bedding for Mrs. Brown _____   Nat. Register No._____

CHRISTIAN NAME.	M. d. W.	Date of Birth.	OCCUPATION. CHILDREN'S SCHOOL.	(1) NAME AND ADDRESS OF PRESENT AND FORMER EMPLOYER. (?) NAME OF FOREMAN.	Time with each Employer.	CAUSE OF LEAVING.	DATE OF LEAVING.	EARNINGS.	OTHER.
Husband			Cripple with arthritis bedridden					₤4/7/6	
Wife								₤1/10	
Son							₤15 done f/week		

FIGURE I

No. of Rooms ....

Rent .... 13/3.

Stand st ....

Rates ....

Rent due ....

Hire Purchase ....

H.P. arrears ....

Pawn tickets ....

Other Debts ....

....

Friendly Society	....
Sick Club	....
L.P.M.S.	....
Trade Union	9 d.
Hospital Saving Association	....
Burial Insurance	1/6 ....
Endowment Insurance	....
Other weekly expenses	....

N.H.I. 1/10 Rates.1/3.
Dr.'s Visits 5/- /
Nursing + Red.K 4/4. -
Medical Necessities 6/-.

NATIONAL HEALTH INSURANCE.

Name.	Name of Society.	Membership Number.

SERVICE PARTICULARS.

Date of enlistment ....

Date of discharge ....

Rank .... No. ....

Regt. or Port Division ....

Unit ....

Date of Marriage ....

Place of Marriage ....

Army Pension or Reserve Pay ....

Army Allowance ....

Civil Pension ....

Public Assistance ....

National Insurance { Health .... / Unemployment .... }

Assistance Board ....

School Meals or Milk ....

Borough Council ....

Church ....

Friendly Society or Club ....

Relations ....

Any other source ....

Total from all sources ....

Net Income ....

Savings ....

TURN OVER

was to be used to take down the statement of the applicant (this consisted of the applicant's description of the problem together with some comment by the visitor; the following comment from a C.O.S. case of 1922 is atypical of a much earlier period only because of its disarming frankness: 'Applicant is a youngish looking man and appeared respectable. I was not altogether taken with him, but this is only an impression not based on anything'). Each applicant was to be given a number to be entered in the Record Book. A Decision Book was to be used to record decisions, which later were also entered in red on the case record, Mowat (1961, p. 29) notes that besides the Visiting Form there were forms for subscribers, for reports to subscribers, for enquiries to schoolmasters and to employers.

This phase—of great practical detail and of the diary-type entry—can be used to illustrate a tendency in social work recording which is not particularly confined to any one period of time, namely the description of what Sheffield has called 'behold-me-busy details'. Some idea of the kinds of detailed records as well as the nature of a social work record in this phase can be obtained from the account on pp. 10 and 11 of an actual record taken from material collected for a study to which reference has already been made (Timms, 1961).

The case was originally referred in 1937, but the record is typical of those made in the C.O.S. in both earlier and later periods. The particular episode on which our attention will be focused concerns a further referral in December 1945 when a social worker asks the C.O.S. to help Mrs Brown with bedding. The front sheet is completed again as shown in Figure 1.

The third phase of social work recording concerns the process record. According to Hamilton this was in high favour in America in the second half of the 1930s, and it has for some time in Britain been accepted as playing an essential part in the professional education of the social worker, even though it has never been practical as a regular mode of recording day-to-day work. Its fairly widespread use owed something to psychoanalytic theory and something to the invention of the typewriter. A process record attempts to present an account of the interaction between social worker and client as this develops in the course of an interview. It differs from a verbatim record, which attempts to present a total recall of an interview, since the primary focus on the flow of the interaction entails considerable selection. The process record is often fairly lengthy since it involves reporting both sides of an interaction and the significant cues to which the worker, on the one hand, and the client, on the other, are responding. For an example of a process record see the Appendix, which contrasts three different forms of record (electric, process and summary) used for the same material.

The fourth phase of recording represents in one sense a compromise. Each phase offers some advantages, though the simple register would now be seen as the basis for some general statistical description of the agency's caseload rather than a self-sufficient part of work with any particular client. The emphasis in the fourth phase is on differential recording. A narrative approach is usual but the liberal use of the summary makes the record more manageable. At the same time particular parts of the work can be recorded as process; for example, the first contact or any particular interview that appears particularly puzzling or fruitful. The flexible character of this phase of recording is well described by Hamilton (1946):

> Applications or early interviews are often given in the client's own words or in a selective process; later interviews, only when the interplay is subtle or unusually significant. Ability to make diagnostic and evaluation comments may provide an effective short-cut instead of full-length verbatim. A whole series of treatment interviews may be just as effectively summarised as the

facts of social study. Interviews in which the emotional values are minimal, or when the anger or aggression or fears are obvious, or in which the case work relationship is not involved to any great extent, or when social resources are realistically utilised by self-directing clients, or when information is sought on a straight question-answer basis, all this and much else can be condensed, arranged and summarised ...

So far in this section I have tried to describe four phases of recording in social work. It is probably the case that examples of each phase could now be found co-existing at the same time in the same county and even in the same agency. Historical research does not help us to discern the beginnings and the ends of each phase. In so far as actual records have been studied they have been used to illustrate a type rather than prove an argument; it is, incidentally, precisely in this way that case illustrations are used in social work texts. Broadly speaking, however, the phases that have now been identified represent some important shifts in ideas about what constitutes a good record, even though existing studies are silent on the developments of recording in work other than social casework.

It is also important to attempt to view the development of recording within the context of changing attitudes to the practice of making records. These are obviously complex, but for purposes of illustration two aspects will be mentioned: changes in the social worker's realization of the impact of investigation and changes in the value attached to recording.

The C.O.S. considered a proper investigation of a case to be of the utmost importance. The 'facts' of a case—and the range of significant facts appears extremely limited to modern eyes—had to be discovered to detect the undeserving and to form a possible plan of help. Ribton Turner, the first secretary of the C.O.S. or, as it then was the Society for Organising Charitable Relief and Repressing

Mendicity, describes (in the *Charity Organisation Reporter*, 31 January 1872) an early instance of investigation after he had seen a man and woman outside his house singing.

> The tune was 'Home Sweet Home', but he believed the words were those of a begging petition. He spoke to the girl ... She said she was formerly at the York Tavern. He asked her if she was prepared to go into service again. She said 'no' ... He found from enquiries made that the girl had not been in the situation (at the York Tavern) for two or three years; but at the last situation she held she had been accused of theft.

In these early days of the C.O.S. the record was seen as a collection of evidence that would justify a decision and describe very briefly the way help was given. In this perspective the applicant was seen in the passive role of informant or as executor of the casework plan: only very limited aspects of his or her behaviour needed to be recorded. On the other hand, it seemed important that the applicant should know that his statements were being recorded. Mrs McCallum in a discussion of a paper prepared for the Council of the C.O.S. in 1895 ('How to Take Down a Case') firmly expressed the view that the case paper should not be kept out of the applicant's sight; facts were going to be recorded and it was preferable that this should be done straightforwardly in front of the applicant. Slowly the emphasis on evidence weakened and questions of the professional relationship between client and social worker came to be considered paramount. This change of focus had a noticeable effect on attitudes to the case records. Its existence came to be experienced by the social worker as somewhat embarrassing. Thus, in 1947 a medical social worker stated that the interviewer 'writes down nothing of intimate personal detail in his (the client's) presence, she keeps record cards and case papers out of his sight and knowledge as much as possible' (Snelling, 1947). Such a viewpoint raises some interesting questions concerning the client as a full participant in any helping process.

As the social work record became less valued as evidence a tendency developed to regard recording as a kind of incidental, mechanical extra. Such an attitude is not unknown at the present time, but it seems to be found first in the early years of this century. Case papers, according to one writer (Lawrance) in 1912 'are the mechanical side of case-work—not casework itself'. At a slightly later date Attlee, when he was educating future social workers, recorded his opinion that 'Visiting people in their own homes is a good experience ... a little general conversation before putting questions will assist in enabling the visitor to get some idea of the kind of person she is visiting ... The filling up of case-papers is merely a matter of accuracy' (Attlee, 1920). Such a view of recording did not receive much support in the later literature which has, on the whole, repeated (rather than examined) Bristol's view that '... case recording is, of course, an integral part of the case work itself. Hence, a separation of the latter from the former could not be effected even if it were desirable to do so' (Bristol, 1936, p. viii). When later writers refer to 'mechanics' in recording they have in mind 'book-keeping' details rather than the record as a whole (see Hamilton, 1946, p. 6).

Three texts

The three main works devoted to recording have already been mentioned. The comparison that follows in this section will be concerned with illuminating any changes in ideas on the practice and theory of recording in American social work in the period marked by the dates of first publication, i.e. 1920-46.

It is possible, of course, to compare these studies in many different ways. In terms of style, for example, neither Bristol nor Hamilton can match what to contemporary ears is the welcome stringency of Sheffield. 'Is treatment', she asks, 'ordinarily furthered by the knowledge that a woman is short? Should we do something different if she was tall?' In this section, however, attention will concentrate upon the different ways in which the authors discuss the purposes of recording and the obstacles in the way of the creation of good records.

For Sheffield the record is the social case history, and she begins by stating the crucial importance of clarity about the purpose for which such a history is compiled and kept.

> The nature of a social case history is determined by the kinds of purpose it is intended to subserve. From its sub-ject matter down to the thickness of the paper it is writ-ten on, from the facts to be selected as important to mechanical devices for convenience, all questions relating to it must be decided in this light. The first step, there-fore, in a discussion of the case record is to make clear the use we expect to put this document to.

Each author attempts to meet this challenge by stating a number of reasons for recording and keeping case records. Sheffield identifies three ends to be achieved: '(1) the immediate purpose of furthering effective treatment of individual clients, (2) the ultimate purpose of general social betterment, and (3) the incidental purpose of establishing the case worker herself in critical thinking' (pp. 5-6). Bristol divides the purposes of case records 'into four main cate-gories, namely, their use for (1) purposes of facilitating treatment, (2) study and research of social problems as a basis for social reform, (3) training of students, as well as for teaching purposes generally, and (4) educating the com-munity as to its social needs and to the place of social case work in filling some of these needs' (p. 5). Finally, Hamilton refers very generally to the work of Bristol and Sheffield, without attempting any cumulative assessment of their views or of any differences her own views might make to the received wisdom of the past. She acknowledges the part records might play in education and in research, but gives first importance to the fact that 'The practitioner in any one of the humanitarian professions is obligated to improve his skill in the interest of his clients, and to make his profession as a whole increasingly effective in the public interest' (p. 3).

There is clearly no contradiction between the authors as they describe the purposes to be served by the case record, but there are differences in priority. In particular there seems to be a certain narrowing of purposes in Hamilton compared to the other two authors. This becomes more apparent if Sheffield's third and ultimate purpose is given in a little more detail. She argues that 'the purpose of social betterment should not be thought of as superseding this individual claim (i.e. the welfare of the client); rather should it illuminate the case problem by constantly relating the difficulties of one client to defects or maladjustments in the social order' (p. 15). She then lists several ways in which this ulterior purpose may be served, including showing 'the typical combinations of character traits or of circumstance and character which make for the various forms of dependency' (p. 17). This recognition of the importance of establishing typicality (the social work record is 'a social specialist's report on a typical instance of social maladjustment', p. 15) contrasts strongly with Hamilton's insistence that the record should suit the individual case.

Differences are also apparent if a comparison is made between the meanings each author attaches to particular objectives. Thus, it could be suggested that all three authors see the primary use of the record in terms of ensuring effective service for the client, but on examination each emphasizes rather different means for achieving this goal. Thus, Sheffield sees the value of the record in helping to ensure effective help for the client in the following terms: 'No visitor in a busy modern office can carry in her mind such details of one personal history after another ...' (p. 13). Moreover, workers change and 'a substitute or successor must begin to be helpful to a client where the previous visitor left off, and with as little loss of momentum as possible ... Lastly, when social workers and agencies team as they do today, the client, his relatives, employers, and so on, must be spared the repetition of his story to different people ...' (p. 14). This emphasis on convenience contrasts with the view Hamilton takes of the role of the record in helping the client: 'Ideally, the record is intended to project our observations and findings; to help us check on our observations; to show our relationship to our clients; our role in helping them; to aid us in formulating our hypotheses and to appraise movement, change, growth, or negative and unsuccessful treatment' (p. 9).

Each of the books we are considering pays attention to various kinds of difficulty in recording. Bristol gives more space to the possible impact of investigation on the client than either Sheffield or Hamilton. In her view 'The attempt to secure data which will permit the worker to prepare a rather complete and accurate record of the social study during the early stages of the contact with the client may result in the use of methods which are productive of fear, timidity, uncertainty or mistrust on the part of the worker' (p. 9). Difficulties in recording arising from the different requirements of particular agencies receive no mention in Sheffield. Hamilton recognizes some differences but her chapter entitled 'Agency Structure, Function, and Policies Condition Recording' suggests that she sees the differences almost exclusively in terms of the content of the record. One of her main arguments is that common principles of recording in social work have been established. Bristol does not treat in detail of the influence of agency structure, but her realistic list of the twelve factors that actually influence the selection and organization of material for the case record includes the following: 'The degree of political control and interference with the agency and its policies. The degree to which the confidential nature of record material is assured. The policies of the agency regarding verifications, affidavits, and acceptance of cases. The nature of the relationship with the agency and its policies' (p. 13).

Perhaps of greater importance are difficulties of a more theoretical nature. Of the three authors Bristol pays most attention to problems of accuracy and objectivity. In Hamilton accuracy is mentioned twice and one of these references is in connection with the special requirements of Public Assistance recording. Hamilton is much less puzzled than Bristol about accuracy, since she is of the opinion that 'A trained ear, eye and memory, supported by notes, can be depended upon for reasonable accuracy' (p. 34). Similarly, she expresses no hesitation concerning the interpenetration of observation and interpretation and does not, therefore, build on Sheffield's attempt to discuss some of the problems in interpretation.

In this brief comparison of the three texts on social work recording we can see evidence that some changes have occurred in ideas about the record, its objectives and its problems. These changes also reflect, but to an unknown degree, changes in practice. One thing at least is certain, namely that in tracing ideas over the period 1920-46 we are not following an inevitable progress from poor to improved theorizing.

2
Why record?

In this chapter we shall be concerned with the more or less contemporary discussion of the reasons given for recording in social work. In the following chapter we shall see how far the aims of recording are achieved and discuss some of the major difficulties that have still to be overcome.

Before discussing either purposes or problems, however, it is appropriate to consider, even if only briefly, what sort of thing a contemporary social work record is. Records in social work, as in other occupations, tend to fall into two main categories. Firstly, brief identifying particulars are recorded to form the basis of a broad statistical description of the work of the agency. Thus, social work organizations will publish annual reports detailing the characteristics of their clientele (the number of men, of women, etc.) and of the service they have given (e.g. the number of home visits). This kind of record of the work of agency suffers from two main defects. The fact that organizations often use their own categories for either client or for work means that comparison between agencies is often difficult if not impossible. Moreover, the categories used are often those that lack any rationale other than the continuation of an habitual manner of description.

The second kind of record kept by social agencies is the account of day-to-day transactions with particular clients

(Hochwald, 1952). These represent the accumulated recorded experience of the social worker in contact with a wide range of problems. This experience is, however, recorded on a large number of documents varying in size, purpose and format. Some documents are, of course, relevant only to the work of certain agencies, e.g. medical reports on prospective adopters, but, taking this into consideration, it is possible to make a few rather crude generalizations. Most agencies use some kind of identifying face sheet (which is probably the accepted source of the statistical description already mentioned). Esslinger (1949) in a study of twenty-eight organizations found thirty-two different headings used on the face sheet; some were common to all (e.g. date of birth), but others were used by only a few agencies (e.g. housing or language). Historical data are treated with less uniformity. Some agencies attempt to record a social history as a separate part of the case record, and at one time, particularly in the training of psychiatric social workers, considerable emphasis was placed on the routine collection of detailed information as far back as the client's grandparents. Esslinger found that a history sheet was used in more than two-thirds of the agencies he investigated. This frequently took the form of an account recorded under various headings. He found the following to be most frequently used: family/personal history, social relationships, environmental factors, economic circumstances, educational history, health, present problem in detail, plan of treatment. Other agencies will incorporate such history as is considered relevant into the beginning of the account of transactions with the client. This account is usually kept on some kind of diary sheet, sometimes supplemented by separate records concerning such matters as budgeting or health. The diary is sometimes a straightforward story of events, and sometimes takes the form of selection in accordance with certain headings (e.g. employment). Often social workers are left with a great deal of initiative concerning the form this part of the record should take, but the probation service has for some time used a standard form of record aimed at helping the probation officer to produce both diagnostic statements and summaries of the work at regular intervals.

Even in this very brief attempt to describe the kind of documents that might together constitute a case record we can see considerable variety. It is likely that this variety will be reduced in the future. In the first place certain types of agency are beginning to meet together to produce some standardization. The Association of British Adoption Agencies, for example, has recently produced medical report forms to be used in adoption work. Secondly, the new social service departments are considering how to produce a record that can be used for the amalgamated children's, health and welfare services. Finally, research workers are arguing the advantages of standardized recording systems that will enable us to exploit our knowledge of clients and of the help they receive. Such standardization is to be welcomed as long as it involves a more efficient way of achieving the legitimate purposes of social work recording.

There is no shortage of statements concerning the purposes which recording in social work should serve. Sometimes these statements concentrate heavily on particular aspects of social work. In 1948, for example, the (then) Institute of Almoners listed the following purposes: thoughtful planning of casework, continuity of treatment, assessment of medico-social needs (at first called reports to medical staff), the provision of material for research. The emphasis here is placed upon the treatment of the individual: no reference is made, for example, to the several aspects of social work touched upon in Bristol's view of the purposes of recording. In general, however, we can adopt for present discussion a three-fold division into service, teaching and research, which is broad enough to encompass the different formulations of the purposes of social work recording that have been attempted from time to time.

Service

As we have already seen, the connection between recording and good practice in social work is taken as axiomatic by most writers. Frequently, the record is described as a social work tool (e.g. Hamilton, 1951, Davison, 1965) but this is less helpful in discerning the precise nature of the connection than might appear at first sight. This is because in the language of social work 'tool' carries the force of general commendation rather than a clear indication of particular technical equipment designed to achieve particular purposes. To call some aspect of social work a 'tool' is, more often than not, simply to commend it.

But recording has not been encouraged on any simple view either of the material to be recorded or of the various purposes that could be achieved. How has the connection between recording and good practice been envisaged? Three major themes can be identified and the emphasis of different writers shifts between them: direct concrete help to the client, indirect help (in so far as the first beneficiary of the record is seen as the social worker), and help to clients in general.

Direct benefits

The social work record has been seen as directly helpful in a number of ways. Several authors refer in general terms to the record as benefiting and protecting the client. Thus, Fenlason comments that 'Competent and responsible practice in any profession requires a record. The record is for the benefit and protection of the person receiving professional services' (Fenlason, 1962). The concept of 'protection' is of some interest. It is not always easy to identify what the client is being protected from (except possible 'bad' social work) or the actual means of the protection, but it is possible to see certain particular circumstances in which a record could serve as a protection. In the probation service, for example, information contained in records will play a part in testing a case of breach of conditions that may be brought before the courts. In cases concerning the removal of children from unsuitable or dangerous surroundings clear and full records will often constitute some protection for the child. This was illustrated by a case recently reported in the press of a thirteen-year-old girl taken into care after she had been severely beaten by her mother and some months after a psychiatric report that the child was in physical danger at home. The officer in charge of the department was reported as being in some difficulty in explaining why the child had been left in the home, because the child care officer who had dealt with the case had left the department; there could, she said, have been elements in the assessment of the case that had not been recorded in the case papers.

As we examine instances like this, however, we can also discern something of the ambiguity that qualifies 'protection'. Records can protect not only the client but also the social worker who, as we say in far from neutral language, requires 'cover' in certain situations. This other interpretation of 'protection' is well brought out in Barrett's discussion (1966) of record keeping in the special circumstances of psychiatric treatment under military auspices. He describes the purposes of military psychiatric records in terms of the treatment of the patient and also of the protection of the military authorities (for example, in the event of claims for pension). A recent British case of a disability claim reported in *The Times* (19.3.71) emphasizes the importance medical records have in this connection. One of the judges commented that the case illustrated the importance of contemporary records as a way of checking the recollection of those giving evidence about past events. The contemporary record, he stated, was the sort of cogent evidence to which Parliament attached so much importance in the Evidence Act, 1938.

Ambiguity is less immediately obvious in the other beneficial consequences of the record for the client that are usually described. What, for example, are some of the consequences of not keeping some kind of record? One of these was certainly identified by Edith Neville in an article on Organization in the *Charity Organisation Review* in 1914. 'Visitors leave (the district), and their successors find not a note or a detail with regard to families who may have belonged to the particular church for years, and who, naturally come to feel the tie a very slight one in consequence.' The client, it is assumed, would readily recognize as beneficial the retention by the agency of an up-to-date record of his or her transactions in a number of other ways. Should the social worker dealing with a client leave the agency or if the case has for one reason or another to be transferred to another worker or even a different agency, then the client, it is asserted, is saved from having to repeat 'his whole story' because the story has already been recorded. Mary Richmond (1925) expresses this and similar kinds of consideration in the following way:

> Workers get sick, or leave, but with the record clearly written up a continuing treatment (and to obtain results treatments must sometimes continue a long while) is possible. The society does not have to begin all over again or else go forward on a mis-conception of what the check marks of former treatments really mean. Sometimes a family or some individual in it comes back for new advice and treatment long after a case has been closed. With the record before us in black and white, we do not have to grope around but are able to begin at once where we left off, and build our new treatment solidly upon the basis of past experience.

Again, a client may come to the agency requiring some kind of immediate help, but the social worker carrying the case may not be available. If action cannot be postponed, then the immediate response to the client is likely to be more beneficial if it is based on current information about the client and his problem. This consideration and those we have just described are, of course, based on certain assumptions. In order for the record to achieve purposes like these it would be necessary, for example, that records were continually up-to-date. In trying 'to save' the client from going over material given at a previous time or to another worker we seem to assume that the client is 'telling his story' mainly for the purpose of conveying information in a once-for-all kind of way and also perhaps that there are no problems attached to using information the client has given to another person, even though the client knows the new worker possesses the information. This last assumption is apparent in Gordon Hamilton's statement concerning transfer from an intake worker to another worker in the same agency. A mature and realistic client 'will not object to going ahead with someone else who also seems to have a good idea of what it is all about (an advantage derived from well recorded intake interviews).' How many 'mature and realistic' people are there?

The direct benefit of the record for the client no longer holds first importance in the discussion of recording, though it is clear that clients might well recognize benefit in those agencies that are using recordings within treatment itself. This use offers promise for the future, but requires much more exploration. Alger and Hogan (1967) have found videotape recordings useful in therapy with marital problems: patients viewing such recordings have become very aware of the contradictions between what they say and what they communicate by means of bodily behaviour. In other settings clients receiving casework or groupwork help have derived direct benefit from the social worker's

29

ability to 'play back' at the end of an interview or group meeting the main themes and problems that had emerged. Joel and Shapiro (1968), for example, suggest that 'reporting back' at the end of a group session helps to bring the session to a good closure at the same time as it affords stimulation for future work.

Indirect benefits

It is the indirect benefits produced by recording that have received most discussion, particularly in more recent times. What has been stressed is the connection between recording and good treatment. Obviously, the connection is not quite as close as that between hospital treatment and hospital records where 'the patient's records are used to control his daily treatment and must be added to several times each day' (Dale and Roberts, 1968a). Yet many commentators see a direct and positive connection between recording and good practice. 'It is not too much to say that without effective recording, professional casework is impossible' (Jarvis, 1969, p. 211). What kinds of help is the social worker expected to receive from recording? A number of specific elements have been described.

Firstly, a good record is said to help the social worker to individualize a situation, whether this is in casework, group or community work. Thus, Goetschius (1969) states that in community work 'Recording is one of the most important tools for the worker in the development of his practice and to the agency in the development of service' since, among other things, it helps the worker to see the separate elements in a situation and to discern their relationship to the total situation. The objective of precise individualization is well brought out in Sheffield's comment upon a number of descriptions which fail to realize this purpose, and succeed in 'merely labelling [the] client with adjectives of a general sort' (p. 191). On one of these descriptions—'she seems a nice little woman'—Sheffield remarked 'There must be at least fifty different kinds of nice little women' (p. 193).

Secondly, the record is seen as helpful in diagnosis and in treatment. Beck, for example, in one of the few British contributions to the literature (1948), saw recording in medical social work as serving two main purposes: presenting all available social information that was relevant for clinical and social diagnosis, and recording social treatment in a way which would help the social worker to think more precisely about her aims and methods. Todd, referring to one particular kind of record in work with the subnormal, states that 'The taking of a social history of a defective is extremely important, as in other spheres of psychiatric social work, both for diagnosis and as an indication of the possible prognosis for the patient' (1956). There are a number of ways in which the record is an aid to successful treatment. It helps the social worker to understand the way the client or clients interact with others. Thus, Wilson and Ryland stress that in group work 'The purpose of the record is to understand the interacting process between the members' (1949). Sometimes this understanding is seen as a product of the process of recording. Forder's view is that the very act of recording helps to impress the facts of the case on the caseworker's mind and enables him to catch facts the significance of which he sees later. 'Often the significance of some details is not recognized at the time, so if they are not recorded immediately, they are easily forgotten' (Forder, 1966, p. 129). The problem here, of course, is that details whose significance escapes the worker are unlikely to be remembered long enough to be recorded. Forder also states that the act of recording ensures that the caseworker thinks about the interview. 'Since everything cannot be recorded, even the selection of what is important itself imposes some order on the facts' (p. 139). Lee sees a closer connection between

31

recording and thinking about the case: 'But even more important is the likelihood that treatment itself would be more adequate and at times would move more rapidly if the interpretation of the worker benefited more often by the clarity and penetration which precise formulation in writing tends to develop' (1932).

Other writers emphasize the value of the record not so much in terms of increasing retrospective understanding but more as an aid to future planning. Bristol, for example (1936, p. 183), remarks:

> If the analysis is not available in the record the case worker is apt to wander aimlessly around in the treatment of the case or to confine treatment exclusively to the pressing needs of the moment. Consistent long-run planning and execution are very difficult, especially in complicated cases, unless the worker takes time to sit down and think through the situation, to record the results of this process and to refer back to her plan of procedure and revise it from time to time.

The record as an aid to orderly thinking is emphasized by other writers, though some of these also indicate that the study of the record helps the social worker towards greater self-awareness. Wilkie (1963), for example, was of the opinion that studying records helped social workers to become aware of the elements they were repressing or altering because of their own needs.

There are, then, several ways in which recording is believed to help in the diagnostic and treatment work of the social worker, ranging from the retention of facts that might play a part in diagnosis to the development of insight in the worker. There remain two further broad ways in which recording is claimed to represent what we have described in this section as an indirect benefit to the client. It conveys information to significant others and it assists in the evaluation of a piece of social work.

In the early days of professional social work agency

records or the information they contained were open to others besides those working in the agency. Since then two important developments have exercised a major influence on the use of the record to convey information to others. Social work agencies have reconsidered an earlier view which favoured the fairly free flow of information between agencies, and an important growth occurred in the relationship between social work and medicine.

A report of a committee of the American Association of Social Workers in 1942 indicates the change that occurred within social work on the difficult problem of the sharing of information between agencies. The assumption held much earlier had been that all information should be fully shared between agencies working on the same case. This working rule had been justified on a number of grounds, including professional courtesy, protection against the client, helping the client, preventing 'too many cooks from spoiling the broth'. The committee made the following recommendations, commenting that they sounded trite since they had been stated so often in the past: (a) in general, no agency should allow a worker of another agency to read its records; (b) routine requests for a summary of a case should not be made; (c) any request for information from another agency should be specific; (d) an agency giving such information should confine itself to what is relevant.

In developing sustained contact with medicine, first through medical social work and later through psychiatric social work, social workers ran the risk of becoming fact-gatherers for the doctors and psychiatrists. They have had ever since to work at the task of differentiating their work from that of the older-established, scientifically-based professions, and this has exercised an important influence on the content and form of recording in medical and psychiatric social work. The kind of influence can be seen in the fact that 'unit medical record' is discussed by Hamilton as one of the special problems in recording, and in the way

33

she discusses it. 'Because the social area is so complex, workers using the unit medical record have to subject themselves to rigid disciplines of selection and condensation lest the social material overwhelm the medical. Many doctors, accustomed to medical abbreviation and hieroglyphics will not take the time to examine long social entries ... Social entries should be relevant, non-technical and concise' (p. 139).

Finally, the record is seen as playing a part in the evaluation of work done. This purpose is frequently discussed within the context of the supervision of trained staff, and it is the supervisory use of the record that has received considerable emphasis in American writing. As Aptekar has remarked, the record is a 'compilation, in convenient form, of factual data required for such purposes as reference, reporting and research. The purpose which case records serve perhaps most frequently and regularly, however, is supervision' (1960, p. 16). The use of records for this purpose does at least face one aspect of the problem of the evaluation of social work—how well or badly is this social worker performing? Yet judgments of this kind must be substantially based and be made on evidence that can as far as possible be agreed between social worker and assessor. These requirements have several implications. For example, on which of the three records in the Appendix should we judge the social worker concerned? As in work with clients the direct and joint use of tape-recorded interviews seems to be strongly indicated.

Benefit to clients in general

To some extent this section overlaps those that have preceded it. For instance, it could be argued that good records constitute for the organization one of its main explicit modes of internal communication. Kastell (1962) argues that the need for departmental communication entails that 'the keeping of records and the writing of reports are matters deserving much attention and thought.' Obviously, a good system of communication can benefit any individual client and clients in general. But clients in general become the prime beneficiaries of recording considered within the context of planning. In discussing this context three major considerations can be identified within the literature.

Firstly, records should help an agency to evaluate the way in which it is carrying out a programme of work. Secondly, they enable an agency to render some account of its work to a wider public. As Fibush and Reeve (1959) have remarked, 'Casework has come a long way from recording for the sake of recording.... But recording itself remains a moral obligation to the community as well as a means of enabling the caseworker to carry out his professional work.' Thirdly, social workers are in direct contact with most if not all social problems and their records contain accumulated experience which should be exploited in the solution of these problems: 'social workers, when called upon to give their views, must be able to substantiate their statements and arguments with reliable data produced from their case records. An haphazard and unco-ordinated system of case recording would make this more difficult ...' (Esslinger, 1949, p. 2). That social workers have a problem in translating their experience into useful statistical form is illustrated by the experience of the Family Service Association of America which published for several years monthly statistics based on returns from member agencies. 'However, problems in definitions, comparability, and reliability seriously limited the usefulness of these data and led to a discontinuation of the series' (*Encyclopaedia of Social Work*, 1965).

Teaching

The record as a teaching device is considered indispensable

by some and is highly valued by many. 'The evidence is all there in the process record and this is what makes it the finest teaching tool that we know' (Heywood, 1964, p. 128). It is difficult to say precisely when social work records were first used systematically in training students, but the practice of giving students batches of old records to read probably dates from the end of the last century. This particular way of using social work records has been continued to the present day. Brown and Gloyne (1966) in a study of field-work supervision noted that 'The reading of case records is a common method of introducing students to the service,' adding the observation that 'from the comments of the students this has diminishing returns.'

Records have come to be used in the teaching of social work in two main ways: as the subject-matter of academic teaching and as the basis of supervision in the field. In what ways can records serve teaching purposes in these different but related contexts? Lee, in an introduction to one of the early collections of teaching cases (Sayles, 1932), identified four main uses, to give reality to concepts which might otherwise seem academic, and to assist in the study of three aspects of social work: 'those problems of human adjustment and human relationship which create the need for social treatment', 'the application of scientific concepts to social problems', and 'the procedures of social agencies.'

These purposes would find advocates today, but one of them is contentious (the notion of the application of scientific concepts begs too many questions about the identity of social work as an applied science) and another draws too sharp a line between the real and the academic. On the whole, more recent discussion shows a more sophisticated approach to professional education, but it is not easy to find discussion of the specific role of the social work record. The record tends to merge into a general background composed of such broad objectives in social work education as continuity, sequence and integration. There is little if any appreciation of the possible drawbacks in the use of social work records. One of the most persistent criticisms of social work, for example, has been its inability to rise above the consideration of series of cases.

In the student's fieldwork major use is made of his own recording of the work he has done with an individual or group. This record is seen as serving a number of related purposes. Heywood suggests that we ask students to record their work partly because the recording reflects their difficulties and partly because in writing the record the student begins to bring together his 'thinking' and his 'doing'. He is able to see 'the clues given—and missed—the response of the client to his method of work, what the client repeated or left out. He has the facts and evidence for his diagnosis; he has also a picture of himself as a worker, a mirror for self-awareness' (p. 128). Clearly a great deal is expected of the record. Are these and other possible expectations fulfilled?

It is difficult to answer this question for two significant reasons. Firstly, we have very little evidence concerning the way records are actually used in fieldwork teaching and, second, the use of the record seems to have assumed such importance that it has become 'protected' by a number of theoretical assumptions which obscure the visibility of the practice. These two points require some elaboration.

The actual practice of fieldwork supervision has itself been under-recorded. The little evidence we have of British experience leads to some doubt concerning the effectiveness of exclusive reliance on the student's record. If we examine the detailed account of supervisory sessions given by Kent we can discern at least two major characteristics. The teaching given by the fieldwork supervisor on the student's recorded work seems to lack any empirical reference; generalizations are used but there is no attempt to consider the question of supporting evidence, whether it existed or what might count as good enough evidence. The following are examples: 'I had discussed with the student some of the attitudes found in paraplegics, how they became despondent, often needed to be shaken out of their lethargy, and to be given clear views as to what could be done for them and what they could do with their lives' (p. 19); the student had found she was calling a patient by his first name, and the supervisor thought that 'By using their title you were not only proving that it was a professional relationship, but also that you were putting the client on an adult basis' (pp. 22-3). The second characteristic is to be found in the marked lack of development of any critical appreciation of language. Where such detailed consideration is given to recording a dialogue it could perhaps be expected that a sharper appreciation of words would result. Take the following extract from the supervisor's comments: 'I said that I believed the best caseworkers were the ones who were emotionally drained by their work, and that I hoped the placement here would show the student that one had to have a level of involvement before one could help people successfully' (p. 13). 'Level' is a concept that appears again in the book and is in frequent use in practice, but there is no indication that it requires critical exploration.

The practice of student recording has developed as a by-product a number of apparently defensive assumptions. For instance, it could reasonably be supposed that the supervisor will obtain an inadequate, inaccurate or distorted account of the work if she has to rely solely on the student's record. Such reliance is encouraged in the literature. In groupwork, for example, Wilson and Ryland (1949) state 'Record writing makes it unnecessary for the supervisor to observe the worker with the group. Observation by the supervisor is a poor substitute for record writing by the worker....' A few writers have recently begun to question this assumption, at least in so far as they advocate much greater use of audio-visual aids in student recording. Such suggestions are met by further assumptions that attempt to remove the necessity for any radical appraisal of the use of the student record. This is the way one writer (Feldman, 1957) responds to criticism of the inadequacy of such a record:

> The remarkable thing is, that the student *does* transmit in his recorded material important information about the client and about the role he himself played. It is remarkable, that while he usually does not understand the meaning of the client's production, he does record most important material ... And it is perhaps even more remarkable, that if the student does not meet the client's needs or even acts contrary to those needs, he still records it.

Whilst it is difficult, for the reasons indicated, to know if supervision based on student recording is achieving its immediate purposes, several writers have expressed doubts about the long-term effects of present practice, particularly in relation to recording. Sytz (1949) believed that schools of social work 'are taking too little responsibility for inculcating principles of recording in their training and so students continue, after they become practitioners, to record in a detailed process form.' Similar complaints about verbosity and views on its origins are to be found in fields of work other than social work. Mitchell (1969) regretted the scarcity of the succinct record in hospitals and suggests that 'To a great extent this is because undergraduates are taught that long-windedness is indicative of comprehensiveness and is therefore praiseworthy.' What require elucidation are what can helpfully be described as principles in recording and the respective parts to be played by academic teacher and fieldwork teacher in inculcating these.

Research

The history of social work recording shows clearly that the

39

relationship between social work records and research has been seen as either closely positive or antithetical. From time to time attention is drawn to the material social agencies have collected or to their position as potential collectors of information in the future. On the other hand, this material is viewed negatively as a form of evidence strong enough for research. As Phelps (1927) observed, 'Case records abound with random observations, which are practically worthless, because no uniform plan was used in their collection and classification.'

Perhaps a topic that connects two subjects as notoriously unpopular with social workers as 'recording' and 'research' stands little chance of sustained development, but the issues involved are of such significance that the subject deserves further attention. This will take the form not of an abstract discussion, but of a consideration of a concrete attempt by sociologists and social workers to consider together sympathetically and systematically the potential use of social work records in research.

This subject was discussed in America in the late 1920s in a number of articles in the sociological journal, *Social Forces*. Burgess (1928), one of the leading sociologists of the time, addressed himself to the question of 'What Social Case Records Should Contain to be Useful for Sociological Interpretation'. He reached the surprising conclusion that 'they should contain what will render them valuable for social case work, that and no more.' This was not because this would help the sociologist to do research on social workers who were not distracted by the attempt to be sociologists, but because both disciplines sought, in Mary Richmond's phrase, 'the power to analyze a human situation.' They would, Burgess believed, approximate this objective if social work records made extensive use of the client's own words. This amounted to something of a revolution since it assumed a fundamental change in the basis of the interview.

It is a change from the interview conceived in legal terms to the interview as an opportunity to participate in the life history of the person, in his memories, in his hopes, in his attitudes, in his own plans, in his philosophy of life. Under the legalistic conception of the interview the attention was often focused upon the art of cross examination, upon all the little tricks of technique designed to elicit information which the informant designed to conceal.... Under the personal, in contrast with the legal, conception of the interview, the social worker aims first of all to put himself so far as possible in the place of the other person, to participate in his experiences, to see life, at least for the moment, as the other person sees it ...

Burgess gave five good reasons for recording in the first person.

1 The interview is placed upon the democratic and friendly basis of sharing experience, the worker entering into the inner life of the other and at the same time imparting the wisdom that comes from contact with similar experiences.

2 Each new interview becomes for the social worker an opportunity not only to broaden and deepen his own understanding of life, but also to test out his own intuitions and tentative plans of treatment.

3 Since this form of record provides both a personal document and objective data, the worker on the case, the supervisor, the staff in conference, and the sociologist are all free to make their own interpretation without the everlurking suspicion of how far the record has been colored and perhaps distorted by the personal equation of the worker.

4 The materials are now provided for a diagnosis in terms of the total situation, rather than with reference to a series of unrelated individual problems.

5 Finally, a current aim, I take it, of social work is to

> place treatment upon a frankly empirical, experimental plane, so that both the original diagnosis and the method and technique of treatment may be subject to review in light of the acid test of the outcome. To record in the first person, by preventing futile attempts at treatment, and by suggesting more individualized planning, will make its contribution to this goal.

Two main objections were raised to the recommendation Burgess made. First, a verbatim report did not avoid the problem of selection: 'a mere verbatim report of the client's words is inadequate; ... if the case worker is adequately to portray the whole interview including her own part in it, she needs more skill and objectivity than ever before' (Swift, 1928). Second, the identity of interest between research and practice was questioned (Eliot, 1928):

> After all, there is a fundamental difference between agencies which study and agencies which treat. One of the two gods, Science or Welfare, must subserve the other. For a treatment agency with limited resources and unlimited needs to record facts beyond the needs of treatment or prevention is apt to be considered misuse of funds. In the agencies where out of research flows some cure, or out of cures flow truths, the results are highly valuable; but one is always found incidental, the other dominant, one a means, the other objective. Those interested in each phase will try to impose additional increments thereof upon the other; but sooner or later the decision must be made and the line drawn.

This interchange of view at a particular time in the development of social work illustrates three important *and* recurring elements in the relationship between research and the social work record. First, the realization that social workers are in first hand contact with many situations which require research and are often the sole possessors of crucial information. It was this realization that led Lundberg to state: 'Caseworkers are the great observers of first hand social behaviour and the great collectors of social data.' Second, the appreciation of factors which militate against the usefulness of social work records for research. Sometimes it is the bias of the observer which is stressed. Thus, Moore (1934) records a trenchant opinion that 'Social case records are full of items which are facts only when viewed against a bourgeois philosophy.' Recently, it is not so much the bias that has received comment but more practical limitations. Observations in the records have not been made on any uniform basis (Phelps, 1927) or, more simply, crucial facts are missing (Jeffreys, 1965). Thirdly, the historical illustration shows a questioning of the identity of the goals of research and help.

These appear to be the main themes to be found in the relationship between the record and research. Is there any possibility of movement beyond them, away from either circularity or ambivalence? A number of considerations suggest an affirmative answer. The reorganization of the social services of the local authority has given an opportunity, which is being used, of reconsidering the form and purpose of records. Some research using the information contained in ordinary social work records has indicated how the cumulative experience contained in these documents can be exploited (e.g. Parker's (1966) study on the prediction of foster home breakdown) and this has encouraged social workers to ask how their information can be fully used. The uniform recording of such details as occupation, age, sex and problem will help social agencies to evaluate at least some aspects of their programme.

Information in the record, then, can feed the helping activities of the social worker, but this does not exhaust the latent possibilities of the relationship between research and the social work record. We should also try to develop social work research as a kind of model for social work recording. This can be done in two main ways, Firstly, the researcher's training in accurate observation and clear recording can be used in the education of social workers. Secondly, we can use and adapt criteria that researchers have developed in one particular branch of study, namely the life history. Dollard, for instance, suggests five criteria to be met by this biographical method, and then applies them to a number of life histories, including Freud's history of Little Hans and the Jack Roller by Shaw. Social workers will certainly be encouraged by Dollard's statement (1935, p. 28) on the indispensability both of the testimony of the person concerned and of the worker's interpretation :

> We will make out the pattern primarily through his reports on his actions, inner and outer, and by such observation of his social relationships as our technique permits, but we must not suppose he will be able to give us a *theory* of his life that is accurate, for in fact he can only give us by his speech and show us by his actual and reported action the material on which we may build the theory.

3

Some critical questions

So far we have described 'the received wisdom' on social work recording, but recently the subject has been given some critical attention. The present chapter will be concerned with the main questions that should be asked about social work recording, including some already raised in the literature. These can be grouped as follows: what are the facts about the behaviour of the recorder that should be set alongside 'the theory'; what are the results of keeping a record, what are the difficulties in making one, and what, if anything, can be seen as the principles of good recording?

Behaviour of the recorders

More time has been given to the exhortation to record than to observation of who records what, and how the record is actually used. Yet questions concerning the real function and actual use of records are crucial in answering the question we often avoid—do we really want an information system? Dumas (ed., 1968) has recently asked such a question in connection with the American Rehabilitation Service. He indicated that the answer depended on whether or not the following assumptions held good: (a) that the critical deficiency under which most rehabilitation workers operate is the lack of relevant information; (b) that the rehabilitation counsellor needs the information he wants; (c) that if he has the information his functioning will improve; (d) that better communication among rehabilitation personnel improve organizational performances. What do the research studies so far undertaken tell us of the behaviour of the recorders?

First, creating records occupies a high proportion of social work time. Miles (1965) showed in his study of Wisconsin probation officers that the largest single amount of time was spent on recording and related activities (30·9 per cent for men and 34·2 per cent for women). Frings (1957) reported that similar amounts of time were used in recording in three experimental systems, representing from 21 per cent to 26 per cent of the caseworker's time. A time study of psychiatric social workers in Britain showed that child guidance clinic workers spent 12 per cent of their time on recording, whilst those in hospitals and the local health authority spent 6·7 per cent and 7·7 per cent respectively (Timms, 1964a). An unpublished study of probation officers in two cities in Britain found that on average the workers spent 16·4 per cent of their time recording and 7 per cent on preparation for recording and reading the reports (Brown, 1970).

But are reports actually read and, if so, by whom? Brown and Frings both show in their different studies a very low proportion of time devoted by workers to reading their records. Miles (1965) found that records were used more frequently than he had anticipated in the following ways: 'as a guide to the facts of case activity'; to help in the fairly smooth transition from one worker to another; to organize thinking about a case and as a guide to the supervision of offenders. There was, however, very little use of records by representatives of other agencies or by administrative personnel in the agency. The latter used slightly less than 7 per cent of the experimental records in nine months and when they did they were searching for specific information.

In professional supervision there was greater reliance on discussion with the worker than on reading the record. Kogan and Brown (1954) found little use made of records in the formation of a treatment plan, but, in contrast with the study by Miles, the record was seen as a product largely for use by the supervisor.

So far we have been concerned with explicit use, but the implicit functions that could be served by recording also require consideration. For example, frequent reference is made to the lengthy and repetitive nature of social work recording, but records may be bulky for reasons other than the simple persistence of the habits of student days. Wilkins and Chandler (1965) suggest that 'It is generally believed by social workers that the more information they have about the cases with which they are concerned the better are the decisions they are able to make', but we know almost nothing about the amount of information social workers can use or the way in which they use it to reach a decision. Rosenblatt and Mayer (1970), noting that decisions may be reached on only a few facts, have argued that the amassing of information serves an important implicit purpose. It helps to avoid or to postpone action and keeps the worker occupied in a seemingly useful, 'scientific' activity, thus reducing his uneasiness in the fact of complex problems.

The results of keeping a record

It is easy to take 'the record' for granted as an obviously sensible and effective way of remembering business transacted between a social work agency and a client. What has been neglected in the past is the way in which the record plays a direct part in the relationship between social worker and client. This takes a positive and a negative form. Positively, the record is an account of the past which the client is sometimes eagerly searching to reconstruct. This can be

47

seen most clearly in the case of adolescents who may have spent a considerable part of their early lives away from their parents. A social worker in contact with them may need to 'paint in' with care and imagination the missing parts of the story—the kind of person a father was; the place in which early infancy was passed. If this cannot be done it is likely that some kind of blank will remain. Mattinson (1970, pp. 30-1) has illustrated these lacunae in the case of subnormal adults trying to recall and recapture some hints of what their lives must have been like. In instances like this a good record would have been of considerable help.

> The File
> Mother: deserted
> Father: not known
> Childhood: Children's Home; sent to Stipplefields ⸱(school) at six years by Poor Law Guardians (1925)
> 'No, I don't know my story. I only wish I could find out. I very often think about it. I don't even know where I was born. There's something mysterious. I don't even know me mother or father or if they are living. I never had a photograph of them—never had nothing.'

The record can also have a negative effect on the relationship and in two main ways. First, the social worker—at least in the early stages of training—may experience discomfort at the fact that records are kept. A great deal of stress is laid on the personal relationship of social worker and client even though this is in a professional context. The social worker may feel this is incompatible with keeping a record, and must reach some solution of this problem. Such a problem is capable of resolution but it is frequently glossed over. Hence a good description of the problem is rare. The following description from a novel captures *some* of the dimensions even though the social work record is more a public than a private document. The main character has begun to write a full account of conversations with

Hugo: 'Of course, I didn't tell Hugo about this. I intended the thing as a private and personal record for myself, so there was no point in telling him. In fact, I knew in my heart that the creation of this record was a sort of betrayal of everything which I imagined myself to have learnt from Hugo. But this didn't stop me. Indeed, the thing began to have for me the fascination of a secret sin' (Iris Murdoch, *Under the Net*, 1954, p. 70). This may seem hopelessly exaggerated when applied to social work recording but it is worth noting Forder's view that 'many clients might be extremely anxious if they realised the fullness with which social caseworkers record what is said to them. It is not surprising that certain caseworkers themselves sometimes feel doubts about whether in this matter they are behaving with complete honesty and integrity' (p. 139).

Second—and this is quite a recent perspective—'the record' can carry all the overtones of 'the dossier'; it can be seen as a powerful influence moulding the behaviour of people. The record can be experienced as containing the client's identity. Goffman (1961) perhaps expresses this point of view most clearly and dramatically: speaking of 'the record' in the psychiatric hospital he says, 'This dossier is apparently not regularly used, however, to record occasions when the patient showed capacity to cope honorably and effectively with difficult life situations. Nor is the case record typically used to provide a rough average or sampling of his past conduct. One of its purposes is to show the ways in which the patient is "sick" and the reason why it was right to commit him.' Again, in the field of crime Kitsuse and Cicourel (1968) have stated that an offender's record 'may never reflect the ambiguous decisions, administrative discretions, or accommodations of law enforcement personnel.'

Difficulties in recording

Before discussing some criteria for good recording it is useful to appreciate the role of attitudes in minimizing the difficulties implicit in recording. The situation in social work recording resembles in this respect that in hospital recording. As Dale and Roberts (1968a) have remarked: 'Errors in medical reports are seldom discussed, perhaps because methods of reducing the errors have not been available, and have not been the subject of papers until recently.' In social work discussion it seems often to be assumed that recording is a relatively straightforward affair, if only social workers would make the effort. Bad reporting, suggests Kastell (1962), may be due to lack of appreciation of the value of a good report: it takes time to write a good report and is less rewarding than making a visit. A good report, she continues, necessitates differentiating important material from that which is not so, and objectivity. In a more historical mood Stone and Kerschner (1959) have stated that 'as we have grown to understand people better, and as our interviewing skills have become more refined, our records have kept pace in reproducing the interview itself.' Such a generalized and positive account of developments in social work is not uncommon. It is common to find no complementary recognition of the need for some evidence to support the optimism.

Some writers, of course, admit and describe the central difficulties in recording, but, sometimes problems are admitted only in so far as there is a solution to hand. Gordon Hamilton, for example, agreed 'That for scientific appraisal these records are incomplete, inaccurate, and subjective is undoubtedly true. Even for practice records may be stereotyped or biased. Laboratory tests of accuracy in recall will always show so high a percentage of errors as to suggest that incidents or interviews reported after the event are not dependable' (p. 156). However, she retained confidence in the record as (inevitably) a tool which in the hands of a skilled practitioner became an instrument if not of precision, then at least of pragmatic value. Her confidence rested on the following factors: the growing habit of note-taking and of direct quotation of phrases actually used by the client, and the repeated impact of a sequence of interviews all carefully recorded. But this is not so much a solution of the problem as re-siting it at a different point in the sequence. The same difficulties that arise in connection with precision, error and so on in social work records are to be found in note-taking, direct quotation and, obviously, in the assessment of a series of interviews.

Difficulties in making a record are considerable and they are of different kinds. Some commentators, for instance, noting that 'Most trained workers confess they are not adept in recording and feel considerable resistance to it' (Dwyer and Urbanowski, 1965), have suggested that the most serious difficulties are not in the actual writing of the record. Hamilton saw the problems more in the thinking that should precede the recording. 'If we can think clearly about the client's needs, his circumstances, and the treatment or movement, the record will shape itself easily and simply' (1946, p. 8). Other writers suggest that the basic problem is to be found in the worker's or the agency's lack of clarity about the general purposes to be achieved by social work methods. Panner and Peterson (1936) suggest that one of the most important questions to be asked is 'Do the content, form, and use of the case record *actually* contribute to an agency's particular purposes of meeting the needs of the people served?' In groupwork Wilson and Ryland (1949) suggest that the writing itself is not the problem. 'Thinking, hearing, seeing and feeling are the problems to be faced in developing the skill of record writing ... the individual who has developed the skill of social group work practice is able to write adequate records, but he cannot write such records unless he has the skill of practice.' We have seen earlier in this book other statements describing the close connection between good practice and recording, but presumably those social workers who record inadequately or not at all remain unconvinced, and what evidence is there that their practice is in consequence poor? Other writers argue that the problems of recording would largely be resolved if social work was more closely related to theoretical considerations. For example Hurwitz (1956) argues that the question of what to put into groupwork records 'would not arise were group work practice more systematic and theoretically guided.' Group leaders without such a frame of reference 'tend to try to follow all the social processes as they occur in the group and to record their observation.'

These, then, are some of the difficulties in recording that have been described. In this section, however, we shall be mainly concerned with the criteria for good recording. Several attempts have been made to state these. Taylor (1953) quotes a Public Health Conference which suggested that the information collected should be (a) not only useful but actually used, (b) valid, (c) significant for the purpose it is supposed to serve, (d) readily available and (e) justify the time and expense involved in collection. Sheffield (1920) placed great stress on relevance for treatment. Thus, in discussing the criticism (to be found also in other work on recording, that social work records often lack 'colour', she draws a distinction between relevant and irrelevant colour. 'Not picturesqueness but precision is what she (the social worker) should strive for; not amateur "portrayal" such as imputes a connection between full lips and warm emotions, close-set eyes and jealousy, erect carriage and pride, but professional interpretation, that chooses its words responsibly' (p. 190). Other writers have concentrated on the criteria of the good record from the perspective of the treatment process. Sytz (1949), for example, judged that records should (a) be of use in understanding and in directing this process; (b) show the quantity and quality of the thinking of the caseworker or groupworker about the professional problems which are his concern; (c) show the skill or lack of skill of the practitioner; (d) show forward or regressive movement or lack of movement, thus revealing, partly at least, success, partial success or failure in helping the individual-with-a-problem or the group.

From these and other attempts to establish criteria for recording two elements require more detailed consideration —objectivity/accuracy and usefulness.

Objectivity/accuracy

Objectivity in recording has been a proposed criteria for quite a long period in the history of social work. A student writing of 'Charity Organisation Society Case-work' in 1928 made the following observation in connection with objectivity. 'That wicked old case-front ... that wasn't sheer cold-blooded rule-of-thumb Nosey Parkerism as they told us at the School of Economics, after all. It was a methodical attempt to draw a sketch of a human situation *independent* ... of prejudices, preconceived ideas, reactions, and impressions.' The student went on to say that she worked 'long enough in a C.O.S. office to get the feeling of objectivity about human affairs, other people's and my own.' These brief statements show at least some of the difficulties involved in the attempt to set objectivity as an aim in social work recording. The personal recorder who uses no audio-visual aids cannot present a view that is independent in the way described simply because he cannot receive such a view. He must observe in a selective way. To be told simply to collect the facts is to be invited to mental paralysis. As Darwin once noted 'Every observation is for a point of view or against a point of view.' What matters are the points of view and the ability to recognize when an observation is in its favour or not. Something of

53

this position was appreciated by Bristol (1936). She was of the opinion that someone who had no theories or ideas regarding causal or other relationships between social phenomena could not be objective in selecting material. 'She can only approach objectivity by avoiding any selection.' Similarly, someone with only a limited range of theories cannot be objective, 'for these limited ideas will constitute prejudice which will in turn restrict her ability to select material impartially. For instance, the individual who believes that poverty is the result of personal incapacity of the client will fail to appreciate the influences of those deep-seated environmental factors over which the client has no control' (p. 35).

Records made by people in the service professions are subject to two major faults: they can make permanent a distorted picture of the interview and they can fail to record important data. The possibility of distortion has been noted in many fields of personal service. In psychiatry Brody *et al.* (1951) have commented upon 'the influence of conscious and unconscious screening in the therapist himself. The incoming sensory material often is neither adequately nor completely recorded.... Omissions, distortions, elaborations, condensations and other modifications of the data occur, and these all contribute to the difficulty of evaluating what really happened.' A study of a total of ninety case reports from three psychologists concluded that the 'findings tend to re-emphasise the presence of individual bias in the reports on the personality of patients, thus raising a serious question about the objectivity of methods of evaluation and prediction if they must rely solely upon psychological reports for this basis' (Robinson and Cohen, 1954). Froelich's study on counselling interview reports (1958) tended to confirm the results of an earlier study that a large amount of material is lost, but that what is recorded is accurate. The question of the loss of material consequent upon the adoption of a particular method of recording is of considerable importance. The Appendix contains three reports on the same interview by the same social worker. The first is the tape record of the interview, the second a process recording (at a later date), and (on yet another occasion) a summary record. These records cannot, of course, prove anything, but they are offered as an illustration of the kinds of loss of information that can be incurred and also as an example of the kind of exercise students might find useful in learning more about recording. Wilkie (1963) has described the results of comparing a small number of cases that had been both tape recorded and process recorded. The main source of distortion arose from omission of the client's statements. The workers, apart from consciously leaving out data they considered useless, also unconsciously omitted to record certain statements of feeling on the part of the client. Some of these feelings were known to the worker but were perhaps particularly difficult to acknowledge at that time. Other feelings were less familiar to the worker because they were more complex.

Usefulness

Records, we are told, are for use. To whom should they be useful, and for what? Some social workers see their record primarily as a set of treatment notes for their own use. Other people, they say, may not be able to make much sense of them, but they can. To some extent they could appeal to the literature in justification, and not primarily because writers from Sheffield onwards have stressed the use of records. The theme they could derive some support from is that stressing the individuality of the record—it must suit the client and it must allow the worker to develop her own style. Yet there is a more important sense in which the record is for someone other than the recorder. One of the earliest articles on recording (Farrar, 1906)

55

stated that 'the record must not only serve to recall vividly to the observer at any subsequent time the disease—picture which the patient presented when the examination was made, but it must also be to such an extent appreciable to any third person, that the latter can, without having seen the patient form an approximate idea of the condition described.' The 'third person' is important because he, as it were, signifies any administrative uses of the record and because writing a record in this perspective helps the recorder to objectify himself and his client.

Usefulness is perhaps the criterion most responsible for the stress at least since Gordon Hamilton on some kind of summary recording. She noted a number of kinds of summary—social histories, diagnostic summaries, periodic summaries, treatment evaluations, evaluation of a foster home, transfer summaries, closing entries, and also case abstracts from other records (p. 46)—but attention has more recently been focused on diagnostic recording. 'The record then is, in essence, a summary of his (the worker's) diagnosis and the treatment steps that have been taken. It is recognized that some supportive evidence may be necessary but in good diagnostic recording the detail, the repetition of like incidents, the trivia, and the obvious activities can be shed, with literal saving of hundreds of pages' (Little, 1949).

Clearly a record is likely to be used if it is relevant for treatment and if it is as economical as possible without loss of significant detail. Reference has already been made to the opinion that social work records are verbose. Reducing any such verbosity would increase the usefulness of the record by decreasing the likelihood of the reader's irritation. But redundancy in a record is sometimes a difficult matter to judge. The following extract from Sheffield (1920, pp. 114-15) gives one authority's judgment on the redundancy in two extracts. It is included so that the reader can test the extent of his agreement with the author, and also as an indication of another exercise in learning about recording which students may wish to attempt on other samples.

May 20, '10. Visitor talked with employer who says (Mrs S. has been thoroughly inefficient and unsatisfactory.) They have not been able to rely upon her either in keeping her hours, or the correct use of her time, or (satisfactory) execution of her duties. She has asked (many) favors, and seemed to think that she was abused when not granted them. She is a (great) gossip, and has created a spirit of complaint among the employees in her section. She (is also constantly) complaining of her health, and the doctor has told her that her troubles are largely due to her excessive tea drinking.

The passages of words in brackets are unnecessary. If an employee does not keep to hours, use her time profitably, or execute her duties she is of course inefficient and unsatisfactory. The more explicit statement includes the general one. If she gossiped no more than the average, this trait would not have been commented upon, therefore the work 'great' adds nothing. The same is true of the phrase 'she is always complaining.' Substitute 'she complains.' Unless she did more complaining than others, her employer would not have noticed it. Small redundancies of this kind accumulating through a whole record interlard the essential items with impeding layers of words.

Take an illustration from a child-placing agency.

(*The words in italics are substitute expressions; bracketed words are superfluous.)

Sept. 6, '09. [F.P.] Vis. foster mo., M. doing (very) well and fo. mo. feels (sure) that girl is trying (very hard) to improve. Fo. mo. wrote to mo. in regard to M's opening her letter and mo. (had replied telling) *authorized** fo. mo. to punish her any way she saw fit. Said M. had given her (a great deal of) sorrow and she knew that the girl needed (severe) discipline. M. entered 5th grade, is doing excellent work. School is conducted in open air (and chn. have been measured to-day for some sort of warm garment to be worn during the winter. These) *warm garments for winter* are to be provided by some society in X. (fo. mo. did not know the) name *unknown*. M. is now taking (a great deal of) pride in her (personal) appearance, keeps herself neat and clean without so much prodding from fo. mo., and so on.

Again we see the unnecessary and therefore ineffective multiplication of words.

Principles of recording

A number of assumptions are made about recording. Sometimes they are described as principles, sometimes as recording theories, but however they are described they deserve attention. The assumptions that will be considered in this section are the following: recording is a generic matter; issues of confidentiality have been adequately defined and resolved; we have identified and adequately discussed the different kinds of record and their relative advantages and disadvantages.

Recording as generic

This assumption usually refers to the lack of significant difference in recording between the fields in which social work is practised. Thus, Bristol comments (1936, p. 3): 'The impression that recording is fundamentally different in the various fields of case work—medical, child welfare, psychiatric, legal, family, and others—because of some inherent differences in the type of work being done in each is erroneous.' Hamilton takes a similar position: the basic processes in recording remain essentially constant for all fields, though content and, to some extent, style will differ between agencies. In her opinion more differences would be found between agencies than between fields, and between trained and untrained workers than between fields (1946, p. 46). The pressure to describe as many factors as possible in generic terms is considerable: the more social workers can claim to have in common the stranger the case for a single profession of social work. Consequently, claims concerning the common nature of recording, or any other social work activity, should be tested rather than accepted on more or less simple assertion. The claim in respective of recording appears reasonable, but appearances are not enough.

The assumption of the generic nature of recording could also refer to the methods of social work. We could speculate that the processes of recording are the same in casework, in group work, in residential work, and in community work. Again, research is required, but it is possible to speculate about this important question on the evidence we have already. This will at least help us to see whether the distinction between process and content is easily applied and quite straightforward. The evidence to be used will be some existing discussions on recording in residential work with children and in community work.

Discussions of recording in methods of work other than social casework are by no means numerous, but it is clear that recording is considered of very great importance in groupwork, community work and residential work. Konopka (1954), for example, writing of groupwork within a residential institution, says, 'Recording is not a luxury that one can afford only if time is left over, but is the means of a systematic effort on behalf of a child' (p. 114). As in casework, so in other methods there appears to be a reluctance to support any particular kind of recording or to suggest that there is any limit to the influence various factors may legitimately exert on the form of recording. Goetschius offers one way of recording in community work, but suggests exhaustively that systems of recording will differ according to agency policy, support, clientele, and fieldwork circumstances.

In community work and residential work there are special characteristics of method which may influence recording. In the first place, the worker is consistently more closely enmeshed with experiences of direct living: he is feeding or helping to feed children, helping a group of tenants to reach a decision about a rent strike. This suggests that the focus of recording should be changed within the group. As Konopka has argued, 'If group living is to become a conscious part of the treatment process, a way must be found to record the development of group life' (1954, p. 112). She goes on to suggest the need for two kinds of record. The first would take the form of a daily log concerning the group or groups. It would refer to the following: conflict and conflict-resolution within the group; control in the group and by whom; outstanding behaviour and how this was handled; the specific content of discussions. In addition a summary of an individual's development would be made at about three monthly intervals. This second kind of record has special importance in children's work. 'Records of a child's development must in essence be cumulative. A regular review of the child's recorded progress may reveal the need for a fresh full scale assessment' (Ministry of Health, 1970). This was written with particular reference to handicapped children, but it seems to have much wider reference.

This kind of focus does, of course, stem from a treatment basis, and some community workers would reject this. They would be concerned with the development of the life of a group only in so far as it became aware of its political objectives and achieved them. It may be that such a perspective would lead to a particular kind of content in the record and an emphasis on the political process or political struggle. If, however, we examine suggested forms of community work recording it seems that they could accommodate a treatment or a political focus.

Take, for example, the recording scheme suggested by Goetschius (1969). This is based on the following principles: objectivity (if value judgments are made they must be stated clearly); controlled comment, meaningful questioning, imaginative planning, and continuity. He suggests that 'Observation, awareness and recording belong together and form a basic part of the worker's skills and techniques' (p. 111). The focus of observation is provided by those aspects of the fieldwork situation about which the worker requires accurate information. Goetschius sees these as: The environment (physical and social); resident as a group; the committee; services that are or are not available; the resources of the agency; external influences and self-awareness. This last aspect is broken down into individual behaviour, methods of work, social attitudes, movement and change, role and purposes of the worker, and relationship.

This comparatively brief reference to discussion of recording in other methods of social work suggests that propositions concerning the generic nature of social work recording have considerable plausibility. Yet some of the differences between the methods have not been systematically considered for their bearing on recording. For example, residential life affords the possibility of regular, controlled observation. Such differences as these may be crucial in so far as they can affect the relationships that are established with those who are to be observed and whose behaviour is to be recorded.

Ethical considerations

The main question here concerns the status of the information that agencies record: it is always described in the literature as confidential, but who has the right of access and what criteria have to be satisfied before it can be used? A lack of clarity has always been a feature of discussion of these issues. A client, it has gradually been agreed, has the right to know that records are kept, but should not be 'burdened' with this information at the first interview (F.S.A.A., 1943). Forder (1966, p. 138) gives an interesting example of a client voicing concern about the content of the social worker's record: 'does this all go down? All my private affairs ... is it all public property?' The social worker's reply is honest, as far as it goes, but it is of some importance that the significance of the client's question is fully grasped. Some social workers would maintain that the client is basically expressing lack of trust in the social worker and his questioning should be seen and treated within the context of his relationship to the social worker. Others, perhaps more concerned with the possible uses of the material now and in the future, would see the client's question as more realistically based on the political facts of life. Jacobs (1968) has recently called attention to the social worker's role as a 'conveyor of images ... a selective reporter whose biases and judgments determine the extent and kind of information the agency received concerning the client.' If Parker (1971) is correct in his description of a 'right to complain', how can such a right be realized if the client is unable to challenge 'the image' that the agency permanently holds of him?

So far we have considered questions concerning the information that a social agency records about its own work, with a particular person, but are there discernible and legitimized limits to the sources from which information may be obtained? For example, should a Supplementary Benefits Commission file contain press cuttings relating to criminal proceedings against an applicant brought by agencies other than itself?

It is commonly said that the use of information held by the agency is governed by the best interest of the

62

client. This, however, can be interpreted ambiguously. As Whitebrook (1945) noted, 'It is not new to the social worker to work within the limits of client consent to the giving or receiving of information. We do this consistently with medical information concerning the client ... The fallacy in our "concept" of "interest of the client" is in the matter of who is the judge—we, or the client.'

This issue of who judges the best interests of the client has received a new emphasis with the increasing use of computers, record linkage systems and data banks. The Seebohm Report, stressing the advantages of a freer flow of information for more effective help to individuals and better service in general, questioned some of what it described as 'traditional attitudes' to confidentiality. One writer has argued that computer records are more confidential than paper ones (Abrams, 1968), but this is true of the retention of information rather than its use, and important problems of access to information are only gradually being appreciated (Hawker, 1971).

The questions raised in this section cannot be answered easily, but the ways in which answers can be found seem fairly clear. We should work along two connected lines of enquiry, one philosophical, the other empirical. We need to explore 'the right to privacy', asking what is claimed by such an assertion and how such a right, if it is viable, can be vindicated. Murch (1971) has suggested that social workers are not as concerned as they should be with questions of privacy. We also need to discover how information is actually transmitted at present between people in and outside various organizational contexts. As Noble (1971) has suggested, the problem of safeguarding confidentiality *seems* simple enough: anything the practitioner learns from the client is confidential and nothing is disclosed without the client's consent. 'In practice, however, relatively complex sets of rules govern who gains access to what kinds of information about clients, in what form, and under what circumstances. These rules are largely unwritten and, more often than not, discretionary. Within the agency, certain facts are written into the record; other facts, if communicated at all, pass only by word of mouth.'

It is likely that our existing discussion of confidentiality is not only too weak conceptually but also somewhat mealy-mouthed.

Different kinds of record

Records are of many different kinds, but a number of categories can be distinguished. Firstly, a dossier can contain a number of different forms, as we have already seen, in addition to the narrative of the case—face sheet budget forms, health record, copies of correspondence and so on. There is perhaps a tendency in discussions of recording to brush these aside as of little importance. Such an attitude neglects the contribution such forms can make and the criteria they should meet. Sheffield, for example, advocated five requirements in planning a face sheet: '(1) that it should be simple enough for the eye to take in its contents rapidly; (2) that it should keep facts of a similar sort contiguous to each other ... (3) that so far as possible it should include only permanent facts; (4) that it should include only facts which can be accurately stated without qualification calling for space; and (5) that it should be plotted out so that entries can be made by typewriter' (p. 49). It is worth considering such apparently trivial detail for two reasons. Firstly, current discussion of the greater use of statistics in planning services often refers to the kind of information contained on the case front. Secondly, research workers have found a number of problems when they have tried to use such information. Borgatta (1960), for instance, has suggested that social workers resent producing this information because they cannot see its possible usefulness.

Records can also be distinguished in terms of style and purpose. Two questions are of concern here. Have we identified the styles (and their negative and positive results) and can the one record achieve the different purposes? Sheffield identified the topical and chronological organization of the narrative. She saw the topical method as securing definiteness as to the general social factors in the case. It helps the worker to develop each topic by paragraph and guides the worker to the facts of real moment in the case by holding before her certain of the broad social relations which give meaning to this or that particular act. On the other hand it tended to efface the process of investigation and treatment, and lessens the force of the interview as an integral statement that may afford an indirect characterization of the person interviewed. Sheffield saw three advantages of chronological recording. Factors could be recorded at once and thrown off the worker's mind. The important steps appeared in sequence. Finally, 'it keeps together the whole statement of any person interviewed, thus giving a total impression of his reliability or bias as a witness'. The disadvantages of this style were that it made for a succession of relatively short entries and workers tended to be careless about introducing irrelevant material when dictating without headings to force the analysis of information gathered.

The topical style of recording is now perhaps less used, though we have no empirical evidence that would indicate the extent of its usefulness. Hamilton discussed three kinds of recording—narrative, summary and interpretation—and topical was not amongst them. She discussed the various ways in which records might be written, commenting in her preface that in 1935 process was favoured but that by 1946 summary, selection, diagnosis and evaluation was in favour. She seems to lean towards narrative in a condensed form with fairly frequent summaries, which may include new material as well as that already in record. She comments fully on each type, giving illustrations, stating that one or all may be used in any record. What is most certainly excluded is an unwieldy verbatim record or a chronological narrative containing no interpretation.

So far we have considered the different verbal forms a record may take, but differences are of importance between the methods of social work and the different purposes that can be achieved within all of them. So we should ask what difference is there between records, say in casework and in community work, and between records with administrative purposes in mind and those with treatment purposes.

One of the best ways to consider any differences stemming from a difference of method is to study a detailed exposition from any method other than casework, since, as we have seen, this method has permeated the discussion of recording from the start. It is, unfortunately, difficult to find such expositions, but Goetschius (1969) has recently described one in community work.

It is clear that he gives to recording a value similar to that accorded to it in social casework. 'Recording is an important part of the fieldwork process. It is a necessary ingredient for in-service training and in the supervision of community work. It is fundamental to the development of fieldwork, its adequate evaluation and interpretation' (p. 111). There is also a similar emphasis on legitimate differences in recording according to agency policy, supporting elements, clientele and fieldwork circumstances. The principles of recording listed by Goetschius appear to be compatible with or the same as those enunciated by writers on casework recording: objectivity, controlled comment, meaningful questioning, imaginative planning, and continuity. It seems that it is mainly in the areas observed that differences appear. The focus of community work will often contain recorded observations of group interaction (say in a committee), of the interaction of the worker with a significantly powerful individual in the locality, and of the impact of social institutions on the particular locality.

We have seen that a great deal is expected of social work recording. It has been seen as serving a number of purposes—administration, treatment, research. Can one kind of record achieve these purposes simultaneously? Writers on this question have answered both negatively and positively, some maintaining that research will always require special recording and that treatment recording is always an administrator's nightmare. Obviously, the answer must depend on the sort of questions researchers want to ask and the kind of information administrators require. If we do not ask too much we can design records which help with the treatment of individuals and record useful if limited information to be used by others.

Conclusion

It would be easy to conclude simply on the note that we need much more research into social work recording. This is undoubtedly true. We need to know about the use to which social work records are actually put and about ways in which their use could be further exploited. We require experimentation with different kinds of records and with different modes of recording. In this connection we would be advised to look, as this book has attempted, beyond the boundaries of social work. Consider, for instance, the possible implications for all kinds of social work of the attempt in the medical field to involve patients in compiling at least some of their own records (Vasey, 1968). But the research will take time and there are improvements that can be made more immediately. As we have noted earlier, exhortation has often been the method chosen to attempt the improvement of recording. Evidence from study groups on recording suggests that this is not the method of choice. We need a more basic and a more practical approach.

First, we should give more time on training courses to direct teaching about and around recording. Several writers suggest that in this country and America recording is either taught on the job or tends to fall between the academic centre and the fieldwork placement. Second, we can do more direct teaching on the problems of observation and measurement. As was suggested earlier in this book, research methodology can be used here as a valuable source. Third, in developing a more critical approach to language in social work we shall indirectly be contributing to better descriptions in social work records. Finally, we should try to move away from the assumption that records are a boring routine by considering them within a wider context. Basically records try to tell a story, sometimes of the past, but always of the present interaction between any agency and particular clients, either singly or in groups. Other disciplines have been concerned with how stories are adequately told, in particular history and sociology. Exploring the perspectives offered by these disciplines will help us to see the potentialities of the social work record in a new light.

Appendix

Three recorded accounts by the same social worker of his interview with Mrs G. are presented with three aims. Firstly, it is hoped to illustrate three different kinds of recording—verbatim, process and summary. Secondly, the reader can compare the three kinds of record in terms of the gain and loss of information. Taking the verbatim record as a guide, can we see, for example, ways in which the other recording forms create erroneous or misleading impressions? How much is the order of information given by the client maintained? What is missing in the process and summary, and is it of major importance? Thirdly, it is hoped that students will be encouraged to undertake a comparative exercise of this kind for themselves, not least because it may introduce them to the experience of tape-recording one of their own interviews.

Transcript of tape recorded interview between mother and psychiatric social worker in a psychiatric clinic for children

Perhaps we could talk a bit about how long you've been coming first of all. Oh gracious, er ... This is where my memory fails. (*Yes*) Er, to me it seems for a very long time. Er, to me it seems for a very long time. I don't know—six months I should say (*Uh, uh*) and yet, er, as you know, I didn't used to look forward to it.

You didn't used to look forward to it? No, I didn't used to look forward to it, but now you see I've got so that in a way I do because I know that I can come here you see and unburden myself and so in a way you look forward to it, don't you? You know, sort of, it's something that you can come to somebody, as I said before. You can unburden all your problems on them and not actually worry them at all.

This is what we talked about last week. Yes.

And then you went on to say 'Well I wonder if it does worry you?' Yes, well, the point being that everybody takes their work home to a certain extent, don't they? (*Yes*). Everybody does, um um so therefore you um ... How I react, I was ... I am getting a guilt complex there again. I thought about this this week—um if I don't say to you I feel better—I feel I've let you down.

How? Oh, this is ... so therefore I try to feel better so that I haven't let you down. I don't know whether you can understand that and um since I used to find it very hard to do, but yet I feel marvellous while I'm here and once I've got outside you drop again. (*Yes*). While you are here, it's ... er, it's um all your cares seem to just sort of disappear somehow but once you're outside you're in the outside world again it really sort of hits you. You know you're going back to the same thing even though you've unburdened a lot, you feel a lot better in that respect but you're still going back, the atmosphere is still going to be the same, slightly better but you know but it's going to take a long pull and you're not quite certain um as to how long the pull's going to take and I think gradually um when you get back home it it lasts for two or three hours and then the children, say, will start or something will happen and you think oh for heaven's sake why on earth did I bother going and yet you feel better in yourself. (*Yes*). If you know what ... If you can understand that.

Yes, you were saying last time in fact that you really felt depressed after I left. Well it's marvellous while you've somebody there that understands you isn't it? I mean, I can come here ... you see, I can come here to you and um you're a marvellous listener. It's not affecting your life at all is it, you see? Actually ...

This is what you seemed to be asking last week. Yes, yes. So therefore I can unburden all my problems on you. Were you my husband you'd think 'Oh good grief not again'. You see. I can repeat myself dozens of times and you never get rude or um aggressive or bad tempered, or— you just take it all so nicely and it's, it's a relief you just don't normally get isn't it? It's so marvellous to be able to do this you see and you're a person that I can speak to without having to be spoken to.

Yes. (Yes) One of the things I do remember is that when you first came that this was one of your complaints about me in fact that I didn't say anything. Yes. It worried me. Yes. It worried me because I thought am I saying the wrong things or is it upsetting him that I'm not saying the right things. I wasn't quite ... I always sort of thought of it as, psychiatry as they asked questions and you answered. (*Yes*) That's psychiatry to me. Psychiatry to a woman is where you lay on a couch ... er, relax completely. Now they ask you different questions and you answer them. Um This is psychiatry in every person's mind. This is psychiatry um ... They ask the questions, you answer them, or they give you drugs—is it drugs they put into your arm? and that ... and you reveal things from the past which you normally keep within your subconscious don't you? Er, this is how I thought that it would be and it worried me sick because you sort of sat there. At first when I used to come, you used to sit near the ... with your chair near the door, do you remember and I got that feeling that I couldn't get out? You'd got me trapped because I hate, as you know, I hate hospitals of any kind.

Now I can come here, I'm not in a hospital. To me I'm in a ... It would be like, like going into a friend's home. You can, you can relax as much as it's possible for me to relax and it's a marvellous feeling. If I could sit here all day and just you sort of sat there and just pour it all out, I'd be marvellous but you see you can't, you've got an hour of this feeling and then you've got the rest of the week to stand ... of the battle—so therefore you you try and think all week of the most important points that are worrying you to put to you when I come but yet once I get in here it just pours out, you you don't really sort of have to say anything, and yet I just sort of tell you everything that upsets me at the time. And it's a marvellous feeling you know.

What about the time interval between um our appointments? These haven't always been regular have they? No. Sometimes, well, um it got to the point the other time when you did ... I couldn't get or sometimes I feel that I could do with the help more often. Now and again you do feel that. Er, like the time when I needed help, so I rang. Er I had to have somebody. I needed help I got so depressed you see, you get to this point. If only you'd sort of ... they say ring up Samaritans and things like this. Well I'm not a person that wants to kill myself. I don't want to do that. All I, I wanted was somebody, to which I do to you, is to be able to speak to and confide in somebody actually who you respect and think, er, you can trust as well, you know sort of. It is, it's a matter of trust and respect isn't it, and it's your approach to me that makes me be able to confide in you. Some people you couldn't, um other people, you can. It's, that's the difference you see. (*Uh huh*) But as soon as you get back ... I leave here now and I'll go outside and then once I get back in home and you get back in the four walls, everything comes back to you. You know very well father's going to come in. He's going to argue with his eld you know with Sheila and I know the arguments with the children are going to start and you're going to get sort of all your worries gradually filled up again till the following week when I come here you see and it does help. I don't mean you don't give help—you do. I mean without you, I'd most likely be in X's [the mental hospital] um um other part. This is it, you see, I mean I would be there's no doubt about it. And without this ... well I couldn't do without it.

But the problem seems to be that we have to somehow transfer what goes on here to what goes on outside in what you call 'the real world'. Yes, but you can't. It ... It is as I was speaking to the lady outside. It is with a mixed family. It's what's happened before marriage with my husband being married the three times, me being married twice and the children all being, even though they're all mine, in my way of thinking, they aren't and they all feel this individually and it doesn't matter what you try to do you can't buy love. All you can do is gain respect. You see they've got to respect you, and for them to respect you takes so much out of yourself and you never feel that you can gain enough respect from a stepchild. (*Yes*) It's a terrible feeling. You always feel that you must try that little bit harder and that little bit harder is taking the more out of you. I don't know whether you you'd understand. Er, small things may happen. Mary happened to say as a matter of fact this morning, she said that one of the children one of the children had said to her at school 'we saw your real mummy's sister', which is quite true you see. Auntie Lilly, and Mary said 'my real mummy's at home.' Well, you see, I have had her since she was a baby, so therefore I am her real mummy even though I've told her the truth and never hidden it, and she was really upset about it and she came and she said ... I explained it again all to her, you see, but she won't accept the fact that I'm not and if anybody says any different she gets really cross and violent. Now I have got that aspect. Then there again you'll get them saying well to Jill, the one that comes here anyway, er, well sort of he isn't really your father. Children at school are very cruel to the children and if anything like this has been said at school or anybody's made a remark or anything comes up to differ between them or, if I've bought one of them something different, say one of them needs something you go get, you go out and get it you see but you've got to be so careful because if you get for one, the other four feel neglected, so I've got to take it in rotation and sometimes one of them will need two things you see and and this causes an upset. This is where you get an argument and they think you think more of one than the other and this is the battle you are standing all the time.

And it's part of your concern to be a good mother that in fact brought you here with Jill? Well that's it you see. Well well, I don't know. My marriage is based on, was say a marriage of convenience for the children's sakes for what people said. People used to come home with the most sort of horrible remarks to the children at school and they used to come home so I was sort of free. I, I never really had what you can call real parents of my own and I think when one loves children, to be honest when one loves children so much, I just wanted them to have something that I'd never had and that's a real family life but I try too hard many a time, I try too hard and this is, this is where the problem comes in. You, you find a lot of mothers are very slap-dash and they sort of go out bingo and dancing or anything you know and let the children look after themselves and these children all turn out perfect usually. Nothing happens, nothing goes wrong and yet like me, you can go out say twice a year, you stay in, you look after them, you always make sure there's somebody there if there is an occasion you have to go out and yet if anything has got to go wrong, it always goes wrong with my type of person, which is very unjust.

What do you mean? Er, oh well, take for instance um oh, I don't really know how you could put it. Er, there are people up the street. Their parents go off out. The girls go out with boys. This is a main worry at the moment with the girls growing up. They go out with boys. They talk about permissive societies and they sort of all go out you see. Now I don't want this of mine. I want the girls to be something special. I want, I think I think you can try too hard at this as well. I don't want them to make the same mistakes as I've made. (*Mm*). It's so hard trying to pass it over to them. They think, they're apt to think you preach and this is where it comes in and yet other girls that can sort of, can go out, they can do what they want with the boys, they never get caught and yet such as Bob's niece, who was brought up the same way as I'm trying to bring mine up, the first boy she ever went out with took advantage of her and she's got a child. You know, this sort of thing ... this is just sort of an example of, you know sort of, these sort of things always happen. I could guarantee if I left mine, something would go wrong. I only ever once left them for ten minutes and Jill had burnt her arm. Things like this, you know, sort of, I always er feel because, it didn't bother me as much which is an awful thing because it was Jill—my own, you see, this is where, I shouldn't, this is what you shouldn't say, my own. Er, had it been one of the others I would have been so terribly guilty and so frightened that when Bob came home, I'm always frightened of what the other people think because they're your stepchildren, if anything happens to them, which has been said to me—oh well she wouldn't really—I mean after all it's only the stepmother. (*Yes*) It digs, it digs deep, very deep and it has been said. It was said by a headmaster of a school once and it hits you and it really hits you hard you know and I think so you sort of try so hard to do your best and if it isn't sort of ... if I I battle with Bob to try and get him just to be a little less stern with them and ease up a little bit because he was so strictly brought up. Well, I was very strictly brought up but yet I've had to, you've got to move with the times but it doesn't mean to say that you've got to let them do as they wish. You've got to have a certain amount of authority. You've got to let them respect you and this is what you've to try and do and as I say with the eldest, er, I don't know, somehow I think intermarriage and step-children and all this they lose um a certain amount of respect for parents, you know sort of there is no other way you can put it, and you've got to regain that respect back and people think it's a very easy job and it isn't. It's hard and it's hard on your nerves, you know. I'm too busy thinking of what others what other peo instead of thinking I'll live my life, I'm too busy thinking what other people will think of what I'm doing or what they think of me. I think this is one of the biggest failings and it's very hard. I always try to look at the other person's point of view instead of saying 'Oh um go your own way', I don't you see. I think now what would so-and-so think? This you shouldn't do really but I've learnt through life always to try and think before you say anything. Think hard before you say anything. It's so easy to say the wrong thing and be misinterpreted but you do you get misinterpreted and since my nerves have been bad I'm afraid um I don't think too much and I just say what I what I think and I've always, as I've said before, been so truthful, it's—it's been a bad thing. Had I been less truthful it would have been a lot easier.

You, in some ways, have been rather playing the part over the last few years because it was important for you was it that you were a good mother? Oh, I played the part of a loving wife, which is a hard part to play for any woman. You've got to play the part of being um sort of your husband's mistress, put it like that and, yet the idea of sex revolts you. Now this is is awful really in a way and you can play the part which I do, everybody around us. Oh, Margaret—I'm happy-go-lucky, carefree, I'm not. I am for as long as they're there, as long as there's company. I'll put a face on but it's like being an actress playing a part but even then after they've gone, then you're yourself and when you're yourself and you've had to play a part for all these years, it wears and it wears and I've got to the point where you just can't keep playing the part, you've got to be yourself, you can't keep it up much longer, not even for the children.

We seem to be talking quite a lot today about you on your own. Well I, I came to the point of ... I've always thought of the family. I've always put Bob and the family first, always. It doesn't matter if I've done without meals—I've had meals, say—We've had meals—um Bob will say 'Have you had yours?'—I'll say 'Yes'—I haven't, because maybe I haven't been able to sort of afford it. All right, he's had his because he's been out to work. I'll see the children are all right, I'd still say I'd do without things, make do with things so's the children ... Well I've done this for seven years and I'm just getting to the point now where I, you know sort of, you take a look at yourself and you think, Well you're getting old and what life have you had? I've not had a life. All I've been is a a housekeeper with [tape not clear] I was employed as a housekeeper, this is, this is what I am —a housekeeper cum nanny.

This is also one of the things focusing on you coming here in that you come here because of Jill. Well I owe the child something, don't I?

Do you? Well I do owe Jill a lot really because when my first husband and I were together, she used to see the arguments, the horrible parts and even though she was so small, even now without even being reminded, she can bring them up. She doesn't have to be reminded of them and, er, I had to go out to work as I say from six till six. They're long hours and leave her behind and you'd hear her screaming at the gate 'Mummy, Mummy', you know. I found out afterwards that the woman next door wanted to get on to the Welfare people because she found that Jill had been ill-treated after I had gone to work. This ... I don't know whether I told you this? (*No*.) Er, when she was screaming 'Mummy, Mummy', seemingly my sister-in- ... ex-sister-in-law, used to sort of really give her a good hiding, put her to bed, and that was it until I came home at night. She used to be up half an hour before I came in and half past six she had to be in bed—well I wasn't in till about ten past when I walked in. So, she'd been in bed nearly all day, crying her eyes out had the child. She'd had no play, she'd had no fun. I didn't know this then, as I say all this came out later so ... This could have helped you before and yet I feel guilty about this because it's something that you shouldn't say. Er, I should have noticed this, so really even though I had to work to support her because there was no other means of support, well no other means I would take. You see, I wouldn't take charity from home. I've always got to have that feeling of er standing on one's own. (*Yes*.) And I've always had it and I expect I always will for as long as I can and yet I can come here and in a way I take charity.

Now what do you see as charity? Er, well I can come, you know sort of, I come here and I'm getting, to me, something for nothing. It's hard, so at first, it was awfully hard to take and it's getting better but it was hard to take.

Are you saying that it's still not easy? Well, I feel that I'm getting help and Jill's getting help, but I'm not giving anything in return. Now, if you go to the doctor's, agreed everybody gets paid, but if you go to the doctor's you

go because you're sort of ill mentally er, not mentally—
physically ill and doctors sort of you go down, the
prescription charges and one thing and another, and doctors, on the whole—the doctors that I mean are the ones
that are, er, like my doctor private and, what is it, practice,
the people they can afford they can afford it, now this
to me is on I'm, er—hospitals are run by authorities
aren't they? In the long run the money comes from the
people? (Yes.) So therefore it's charity I'm getting. I'm
getting this money, I know, it's coming so much of it
comes out of my husband's wage—a halfpenny a month
maybe, but or whatever you call it, I don't know, but
it's still charity. To me, it's, you're getting something—
you're getting help—and you're not giving anything in return. Now I felt today, out there, trying to speak to that
lady (Yes) that I was sort of giving something back in
return.

Yes, yes, and this is very important. Well, it's important
to me. It's maybe me you see. I just don't like, I don't like
owing the world anything.

*What about, er, the situation where you may feel in
debt to me?* Yes, well I felt so awful that if I say as last
night, I was ill, I wanted to ring today, I just couldn't
face—I wanted to come today but I couldn't face coming.
(Yes) I felt awful, I did feel awful (Yes) and I felt ill and
I thought no, I'm not ringing; because I put him out, I put
Miss Z [psycho-therapist] out. They're doing something
which you don't have to do, you don't have to do this.
Er, to me a welfare worker is somebody that helps people
that are in need but you're doing a psychiatrist's job. You
are actually doing psychiatry. You are doing as much for
me as a psychiatrist could do and yet you're not getting—
I maybe don't know whether you should do this—paid
the amount that a psychiatrist gets. Now this is unfair
to me—this is all wrong—you don't have to do this—you
go out of your way to help us so therefore I felt, I didn't

want to owe you anything. I don't want to owe anything you see, is not there but (*Uh um*) and it's an, as I say, it's a trait I've always well I've had it for a lot of years and never sort of never just sort of—I don't get any pleasure in, I get a certain amount of pleasure receiving but I get more in giving (*Um*) and I get, you do get this feeling of guilt. You see, I feel that I owe you something for what you've done for me. Now. How do I pay you back?

And will I, in fact, ask? Yes, but this is, this is hurt you know and I didn't like to say it.

Is this also connected in some way, I'm not sure, but is it also connected with your saying it doesn't affect you that you can tell me things and that this doesn't in fact have any great impact on me? I don't know because I've tried to think that out this week and it just won't come. (*Um um*) It won't come at all. (*Um um*) Er, I thought sort of at first, well I'm just a case, I'm just a person who is part of his job, it's like somebody serving in a sweet shop. They come in for a quarter of sweets, they tell you their troubles and out they go and in comes another one you see. This is it. Er, I used to do this, I know. Er, you you ten to one forgot them, now and again there were odd things that stuck in your mind, you know, poor woman, you know, or anything like that. Er, then eventually, it went out, but yet I sort of felt that I could speak to you because you could go out tonight or go home or whatever and, er, you can forget it until next week and then you may think 'oh, gracious I've got to listen listen to that awful woman's problems all over again, the same thing over and over again'—you know this is it. And yet you take it, you take it with a smile and you take it every time and nobody else would.

Um, and in some ways it would make it reasonably O.K. in your idea if Jill was coming and so therefore you know we talked about Jill and that I saw you because Jill was coming to see Miss Z. That's right.

But recently we seemed to have been saying something else don't we? Er, well, you see while Jill was coming to Miss Z it seemed only right that, er, you wanted to find out from me what had happened to me to make Jill like that. So actually this was in my mind.

This is how you saw it? Yes. This is how I saw it. That, er, you were sort of getting my side of what, er, life was like at home to affect Jill in that respect, you see. Now this is how I felt. Then afterwards I wasn't quite sure because Jill has told me that she tells Miss Z things that she wouldn't say at home and she couldn't tell anybody at home and she wouldn't tell me, (*No*) and I wouldn't expect Miss Z to tell me (*Right*), you see this is all right, I don't mind this. Even if it was something terrible I'm not bothered so long as she can get it off her mind you see. So therefore once I found that you'd already known what was going on at home, what our home life was like. I mean, it isn't as if it's a, er, well there can be happy, middle and back street, er, well I mean to say they weren't getting clothed properly, or fed properly or um they were being ill-treated you know, you see, I mean I could understand it, but you know they're not, or I presume you know they're not. So therefore it hit me the other week, why do I still go to see Mr H. [the social worker] when he's not a psychiatrist (*Um*) and it worried me and I thought now what could I do to repay, you see. I've got to find some way of doing a repayment back or else I can't accept it. It's an awful thing to say but I feel this. If I'm given a gift I've got to give one back. It doesn't matter what it is, how small it is, even if it's only a kindness I can do. Er, so they gave me a lift in the car the other day, so yesterday I helped her on the bus with the pushchair and the baby. I didn't feel well I'd been ill all morning but I helped her on the bus because I'd paid her back for the kindness she'd done me the day before. (*Yes*) Now you see it's this sort of thing. I just cannot accept the allowance from home. I was, I could have had, you see, the allowance from home, I wouldn't take it, I didn't want it, I hadn't earned it so therefore I didn't want it, but I believe that Bob keeps me—when Bob goes I earn the money at home, you know sort of he'll go sort of sometimes jokingly and sometimes he means it 'You've never been so well off'. (*Um*) I've been a lot better off in a lot of respects. But yet he seems to feel that sort of I feel anyway that the work I do and the work that I put in and helping him and helping the children being, er, mother, mistress, cook, housekeeper, whatever you call it, laundry-maid, everything all into one, I earn my keep my keep and this is what's kept me there and what's kept us going, the family, you see I earn it. So I work twice as hard to please him, all right, I sort of even if I felt ill and I thought that I could please one of the children say, I hadn't much money and they wanted a birthday present, I'd work all day at something, to make them something so that they felt, they feel wanted and yet I don't want them to ever feel that they owe me anything.

Ah—why's that? Because at home you were never allowed to have anything. Er, when we were brought up with the two maiden aunts you had to work for every penny. I used to have to work, er—walking to school two and three miles and home back for lunch, you know, mile and a half there and a mile and a half back, you know, and the same at lunchtime. In the morning you had to get up early, you had to take the dogs for a two-mile run every morning you know, come back up, see to the horse and the animals, you see. Then you could get washed and changed and ready for school, and nip to the shop, back you know then you went to school again. Lunchtime the same sort of thing. You were allowed then threepence a week but you never, ever, if you wanted to go anywhere at all, Auntie always told me you never get anything for nothing in this world. Everybody pays the price. It doesn't matter what it is you may think you're getting something for nothing. But everybody— it's the same as going into a supermarket. You think you're getting something cheap but you buy all your groceries there and you've ended up paying just the same because what you lose on the roundabout you gain on the swings.

Yet you wouldn't want your kids to feel this? No, no, I want my children to feel a respect, a certain respect for money but yet I feel so guilty that I can't afford to give them what their friends have. I'll admit that, I do admit that but we never, we were taught to respect money but you'd to earn every penny and father, when I saw him, which was very very rare, er, he used to say you've made your bed girl, you lie on it, you see, and he said always remember that you never get anything, anything for nothing, and if somebody gives you anything for nothing there's always an ulterior motive behind it.

You're saying are you that you don't want your kids to believe this? No, because it's a terrible guilt complex and something that you shouldn't have.

So, in fact, you don't think it's a very good idea that people should always feel that they can't be given things? No, I know in my own mind, you see, I know it but can't accept it. You see, I know that you should have pleasure in—other people will have pleasure in giving as much as I do, and I don't want anything back for it. I could give you everything say presents or anything and I'd be most hurt if you gave me anything back. Now this is, this is the terrible part of it. But yet if you gave me anything I'd think 'Oh what's he want?' Now this is it and I don't want the children to get this feeling and Bob like me, he always thinks if anybody gives you anything there's a reason behind it, there's an ulterior motive.

You don't quite rightly want children to feel this? No.

It's one of the ways that you can get them to freely accept things, except in [tape not clear]. Yes. The children you see, they say, er, and the neighbours goes—that young man in the sports car is a lucky young man sort of thing and I go 'oh, yes' you know and we—they make a joke of it you know and Joy and Brenda said the other day 'Do you know, since you've been (this is quite true this is) since you've been to see him or been going to see him, um I don't know what you do when you get there' (because of course I don't discuss it you know). I've told them that I speak to you, you see, and unburden my troubles but I've said that much you know, because we've coffee together but they said you seem to ease off and then by the time it gets round to a couple of days before, you're unbearable again. You see they will tell me and I am unbearable. It gets to that point you see, I get to that pitch again and ... Brenda you see doesn't ... Brenda likes Bob ... sort of likes Bob to be ... speak to him but they see him as he is and he's hard and doesn't give in and he expects to be waited on in a lot of ways hand and foot and they see me running around, they call me the slave girl and yet I, I like work. I like work. I love working and yet and yet they see it, and they speak to him and they sort of accept him because he's my husband but they've told me if ever such a time came, which they must be able to see this, that I left, they would never accept him. They accept him through me and I'm a I'm a bit 'door-matty' you know. Sort of just let anybody wipe their feet on me sort of I'd do any kindness for anybody but to me if it was helping somebody it was worthwhile, but I can't accept the same back and want the children to be able to accept things and to have pleasure in both giving and receiving—nct like me—and you fight this battle you know with yourself and you know it's wrong when you can't do anything about it.

But is there still hope that you will be able to accept things? No. I shall always be the same I know this. I try, you know, I try so hard and even and even to a halfpenny at the shop. Half a new penny, sorry. I owed the, I owed the shopkeeper half a new penny, now this is nagging me now. I'm sat here. Er, I sent the child up this morning. This is nagging me. She's most likely forgotten about it. She does this you know, but I can't forget that I owe her this and well, as soon as we get off the bus that's the first thing I shall do is take it. It's an awful feeling you know, it's terrible.

Is it becoming easier with me? Er, it's becoming easier but not, it's not going. I thought it would go (*Um*) and I thought, well if I could help you in some respect ... or that I was helping you in your career in some respect, I wouldn't feel too bad about coming. But if it wasn't doing anything at all for helping you, I couldn't accept it. (*Um*) And this is it you see, and er ...

Well can we continue to go along that basis for the moment? Yes. Well if I thought that, er ... well if, sort of, if I thought for instance there was anything sort of that I could do that was within my limits as a person to do, I don't know, say like today I spoke to that woman out there, now that's most likely nothing whatsoever to do with you, but if I thought that helping that woman and giving her my number or her wanting somebody to speak to, which she says she hasn't anyone, would help that woman (*Um*) I'd do it. (*Um*) I'd be glad to do it, you see. If I thought that speaking to you and helping you to further your career, or anything that I could do in that respect, I would do it. Even if I didn't feel, even if I felt awful or, er, I don't mind so long as I'm helping, paying you back for the kindness that you've done me. I can't accept that you get paid or that you get a petrol allowance if you had to come to our house. I can't accept that at all.

You don't accept that? No. This ... I went into what a social welfare worker is.

Did you? And it's not this ... Now I can't understand exactly and this has been eating me this week, as to what you are aiming for.

Aiming for—can you expand on this? In the future. (*Yes*) Because you're wasted in this job. Er, I don't know whether I should have said that, er? You've got such a good way with people. I'm not bulling you up, not one bit. This is sincere is this and it annoys me to have to say it—I don't know why. You've a way with people that very few people have and I've met a lot of people, and you've a way with you of letting, of making people—I don't want to ... many a time I come in I think 'Right, I'm not going to say a word to him today'. You know, this is how I used to get you know. (*Yes*) And I used to sit here tense and I used to think it doesn't matter if you sit, I just sit there and look at him you see, and you've a way with you of making a person reveal all whatever they feel. You don't even have to open your mouth, you just sit there and it does, it ... It's just a feeling, I don't know, I don't know what it is. It isn't something I could explain, it isn't something you could put into words you know, it's just there. And to me you're wasted in ... all what I've been reading up on what social welfare is. All right it's a marvellous job but you in your own particular field and in the way that you can make people confide in you, could do better. Am I wrong in saying this? This is my feelings and, er, I just wondered sort of if you had, er, it's none of my business isn't this you know at all, and I wondered if, sort of, if there was anything, you know, sort of, or you had an idea of getting further up the scale. Everybody wants to, let's admit it. But I don't mean it because of that, I mean it because, er, you're a person to me of, I don't know, you've got, you're wasting something that you've got and many people haven't got and you're wasted in a way in that respect.

Of course, if I did change my job I wouldn't be here to see you next week. No, but yet if it was helping you up the scale because you've helped me, I'm grateful. You can't, I'd even, you, you wouldn't see this, er, if I thought that er you've got up further, er, I know it would be a blow to my, or I wouldn't be able to say, say somebody else strange came I'd just say 'Oh, I feel all right thank you. I'm a lot better', you know, and I just wouldn't come anymore. Most likely end up as I say, in [the mental hospital]. But if it's got you up the scale, well I wouldn't bear any resentment towards you (*I really*) no because you're going to be able to help other people that are worse.

I really think you're being rather hard on yourself and you know as long as you want to come I'm going to be around for quite a while.... But the point being this, that you don't have to do it, so why do you do it? Am I allowed to ask that—no.

Because you and I got to know each other and I said— perhaps not in words but I said it—by seeing you that if we got together every week that we could make things better for you. Now I think it's fairly important if I make that promise I really try and carry it out. Yes, but yet ... You've so much other work to do. I've enquired into this. I know I shouldn't have done that. You are absolutely choc-a-bloc, full of work most of the time, dashing here, there and everywhere, and yet you spare time to be bothered with my problem which to me is very big, but to you, I feel to you it's very trivial.

But on the other hand, your kids know that you have an awful lot to do, with the horses, with the dogs, with all the things in the house, but you're able to spend time with them aren't you? Yes. I've even stopped them doing things in the morning before they go to school. I've started doing all the housework myself so that they don't have it to do.

Yes. And they think this is quite reasonable that you should do this? Well, that's what a mother's for isn't it? (*Right*) Let's face it. (*Right*) This is a mother's job you see and I want to be a mother, I want to be a good mother. (*Yes you do*) I've tried being a good mother and I think it's worked to a certain extent, but it's the mother/father relationship that's gone.

Yes. Well, we've got plenty of time to talk about that because I'm going to be around. But it's, as I say, it is important to be a good mother to one's children, but when you find that they've gone astray now and again—it hits you.

But you go on trying don't you? You go on trying and you go on trying but there comes to a point where you feel as if, like I've got you, er, you keep, you keep bucking me up enough to keep going for another week. All right um. If I didn't speak to you I don't think I'd last another week sometimes. This is being honest. (*Yes*) Er ... If I didn't have anybody to speak to, you get to a line, sort of, I get, you know, sort of, that time when I didn't see you were on holiday at Christmas. (*Yes*). You get to this line and it's sort of a line, you feel as if one more, just one more argument and something's going to go bang. (*Yes*) It's a horrible, it's well it isn't just going to go bang, you just can't explain things, you want to throw things (*Yes*) you want to scream, you get on, it's terrible, it really is awful. And you get to this point but yet with you, with me speaking to you every week, relieves my sort of feelings and tension, it helps me to get through another week but yet I'm not going to be able to rely on you. I've got to be independent.

Sometimes I'm on holiday. Yes.

Yes. Maybe sometimes you get angry if I'm away. I was

at Christmas. I'm trying to accept at Christmas you see, everybody's got to enjoy Christmas, haven't they?

But? I'd nobody to get in touch with. Er, I wouldn't have rung—ten to one I wouldn't have rung as you know what happened, well you know all the carry on that went on, but had I had some way of been knowing that I could have contacted you if needed be at any time, I wouldn't unless it was absolutely oh, you know it would have to be the last straw but yet I didn't and I couldn't and I didn't know anybody else that, er, I could trust enough to do it. So therefore, I went haywire didn't I? You see this is it, this it what was it. If you know you've always somewhere where you can, er, get in, you know, sort of in touch with somebody, I mean you wouldn't dream of going in on their privacy you know, unless it was the absolute last straw and by it would have to be the last straw before I did anything you know. This is the point and, er, I got that feeling at Christmas you know, well all right, well he needs a holiday you know and I'm saying to you well don't worry and I'm thinking er you know, I can see it coming off you know, sort of one terrific barney, there always usually ends up one you know sort of, as you know I hate Christmas to start off with. *(Yes)* And I thought there's going to be sort of one barney come up and Margaret's going to end up back in the Infirmary. I could see it coming off and I daren't say it, because I wanted you to enjoy your holiday you see.

When I mentioned before Christmas do you remember you said, er, that it would be all right if I, if you didn't see me for three weeks because by that time you would have been out of your depression. So you sort of did say to me didn't you? I put an act on. *(Yes)* A rotten act but it worked. Er, I'm sorry but if I can help people's feelings by putting an act on—I'm not now because I can confide in you which I have done you see. I can confide in you but even then I was unsure and—could confide in you, no don't get me wrong, but I wanted you, you deserved a holiday after what you'd taken you know. To me, from what you'd taken, I mean ten minutes of me speaking like this and Bob goes absolutely haywire, you know. Er, he's heard enough he can't stand it.

So it is important for us to, if there is ever going to be a break in our weekly appointments, to plan this ahead ... (If I can just ...) *... so that it doesn't come as a surprise.* You see—the other week when I felt—was it last week or some time—I rang up and you aren't always here, you see, you were at the University. So they ... (*That's right*) I needed somebody to talk to. There was nobody there. Er ... I thought well all right he isn't there, you know. He'll be there tomorrow so that, even though I didn't sleep all night and that you know, er, it was all right because I'd only a day to wait. (*Yes*) But you take a fortnight, it's a lifetime if you're nervy or edgy, or you feel that you must confide in somebody over something and you know there's only one person that's not going to sort of laugh it off you see because everything I say at home is laughed off you see. Psychiatry is one big laugh you know and, of course, with Jill playing up as I say this week owing to Miss Z leaving ... Bob ... I think she was better off before she even started ... (*Yes*) ... this sort of thing.

So it is important that if we do have any breaks that we plan for it and that you do know that I'm going to be here in the future. If, sort of, if I just sort of knew that, it sounds silly doesn't it, er I wouldn't you can ring your own doctor and he'll go—'Come down to the surgery tonight'. Say you really—I don't, I hope I never get like that again. I'd get a doctor out, but say you ever did you know come down to the surgery tonight—what good is that to you? You know—I mean I was in tears—Come down to the surgery tonight.

What did you need? Anything, anybody to speak to or anything you see they haven't got the time. A doctor, your ordinary practitioner's got about four minutes per patient. All right, well my doctor the other night gave me nearly three quarters of an hour, only because I think somebody at this hospital had spoken to him about me or sent a letter. Otherwise you get your four minutes there's you see they must do this, there are other people that are ill. Not, not ... You think of yourself, as I said before, as the only person in the world that's got anything wrong with them, and you're not, you're one of a number.

But, what I'm saying to you is that for an hour each week if you want to, you know, you can be the only person. Yes, (*And*) well, this is it. (*You know*) You couldn't get this at a doctor's.... You've got to be ill. (*Yes*) You know, sort of physically ill, it doesn't matter about your mental condition, you've got to be physically ... and if you can walk, you've to go down. You know. I mean you could be bleeding, so long as you can walk or catch the bus, you've to go down. This is it, you see. They haven't —there are always too many patients to be honest to the amount of doctors there are. And, I mean, this is the problem isn't it but yet here I get a whole hour for nothing and it's ...

You're still a bit unsure about it? Yes.

Well, we'll see you next week.

Process report

Confidential

re: Mrs G. Interview on 25/2/71, dictated 26/2/71.

I asked Mrs G. how long it is she had been coming to see me and she said six months. After some thought, she could not remember, it seems a long time. She then went on to say how she could talk to me because I was not affected by what she told me and that she did rehearse what she was going to say but somehow, when she came here, it all poured out. I mentioned a time when she had not in fact felt like talking to me and she recalled that I used to keep my chair by the door and she felt she could not get out. Sometimes she decided that she was not going to say anything but in fact she always did when she came. She said that she felt as relaxed here as she ever did but, when she got outside into the real world and she had to go back home to her husband and she gets so tense looking after the kids. I suggested perhaps we should try and move towards transferring the situation here to the one at home. She said that it was different here in that, if I was her husband, I would shut her up after 10 minutes but she always had an hour here.

She talked about Psychiatry and what she had expected, that you laid down on a couch and the psychiatrist asked you questions. She then said that she thought perhaps she should not have but she had been looking up what social workers do and it was not what I did and it had been worrying her. I said that she had been concerned the other week about how she would be in debt to me. She said that it was not satisfactory, knowing that I got paid for my petrol; she didn't really accept this because psychiatrists got paid so much, she didn't worry about asking for their time but it seems (and here she is playing with her fingers in great tension) that she was getting charity. I asked what she meant by charity. She said that she knew her husband paid but I didn't have to see her. Why do I? I said that we agreed that we would meet every week but that sometimes this had not been regular and perhaps this has been difficult for her. She immediately related this to Christmas—'You know how I dislike Christmas and I knew you deserved a holiday but if I had just been able to get in touch with you, I would not have done, only if it had been very desperate.' Here she is speaking hesitatingly. She mentioned fear of taking another overdose.

It is so difficult at home. In some ways she did not mind the fact that it was Jill that was referred. I queried this and she said 'I should not say that, should I?' looking up at me, but that people always talk about you as a stepmother and expect things to go wrong. I said it was good that she could bring Jill because she was concerned to be a good mother. She said it was difficult as she had had her previous husbands and Bob had had two wives.

I asked her if she found it difficult to come and see me in her own right and she talked again how much she felt she owed me and what she wanted to give me. She said that her father had taught her never to ask for things. She hardly ever saw him and she was intent that her children should feel they were able to give freely and not feel guilty because it is an awful feeling. I asked if perhaps she could learn through me to accept things for herself and so teach the children this and she went on again about how she owed a penny at the shop and intended as it was on her mind to give it back when she went home. She then said that she felt, if it was helping my career, that she would not mind if I left. She wondered what I had in mind because obviously I was wasted. After her talking about this, I said that in fact this would mean that I would leave her and that I had no intention of doing this and we would meet together regularly. She says that her husband laughs about Psychiatry but the neighbours talk about that young man in the sports car that comes to see you and they noticed that she is more relaxed after I left and two days before she is getting tense and I say that I look forward to seeing her next week.

Summary report

Confidential

re: Mrs G. Dictated on 4/3/71.

Length of time she has been coming, how it's kept her out of hospital. My praise that she wanted to be a good mother and her fears about what people say about step-mothers and the expectation things will go wrong. Perhaps influenced by the recording and knowing its purpose a lot about my value to her and spontaneously talks about Christmas, when I mention that she said she would be out of her depression by the time I returned. She talked about how she would have liked to have had the *knowledge* she could get in touch. She talks about my role and her puzzlement that I don't have to perform this service relating it to how she finds it difficult to 'owe' people and links this with her childhood. Is determined to enable her children to receive things without feeling guilty. I talk about transferring the situation with me to that at home.

She talks about my promotion to a better job and how she would like to help. I refer to my commitment to our appointments.

Bibliography

ABRAHAMSON, ARTHUR C. (1955), *Social Work Practice in Canada—Case Records and Examples for Study and Teaching*, School of Social Work, Vancouver: University of British Columbia.

ABRAMS, M. E., *et al.* (1968), 'A computer based general practice and health centre information system', *J. Royal College General Practitioners*, *16*, 6, 415-27.

ACHESON, E. D. (1967), *Medical Record Linkage*, London: OUP.

ACHESON, E. D. (ed.) (1968), *Record Linkage in Medicine*, Edinburgh: Livingstone.

ALGER, I. & HOGAN, P. (1967), 'The use of videotape recordings in conjoint marital therapy', *Am. J. Psychiatry*, *123*, 1425.

ALLPORT, GORDON W. & POSTMAN, LEO J. (1958), 'The basic psychology of rumour', pp. 54-65 in MACCOBY, E. E., NEWCOMB, T. M. & HARTLEY, E. L.

ALPERT, M., HEKIMAN, L. J. & FROSCH, W. A. (1966), 'Evaluation of treatment with recorded interviews', *Am. J. Psychiatry*, *122*, 1258-64.

AMERICAN ASSOCIATION OF MEDICAL SOCIAL WORKERS (1949), *A Statement of Standards to be Met by Medical Social Service Departments in Hospitals and Clinics.*

AMERICAN ASSOCIATION OF SOCIAL WORKERS (1942), 'The use of case records', *Compass*, November, 9-16.

ANDERSON, M. E., PFEIFFER, E. E., SCHUBERT, M. S. & SCOTT,

L. (1953), 'The content of first year fieldwork in a case-work setting', *Social Casework*, *34*, 2, 61-7.

APTEKAR, H. (1955), *The Dynamics of Casework and Counselling*, Boston: Houghton Mifflin.

APTEKAR, H. (1960), 'Record writing for purposes of supervision', *Child Welfare*, *39*, 2, 16-21.

ARCHER, B. W. & MARGOLIN, R. R. (1970), 'Arousal effects in intentional recall and forgetting', *J. Experimental Psychology*, *86*, 1, 8.

ARGYLE, M. (1957), *The Scientific Study of Social Behaviour*, London: Methuen.

ASSOCIATION OF HOSPITAL TREASURERS (1964), *An Enquiry into the Methods of Keeping Staff Records with a View to Establishment Control*.

ASSOCIATION OF SOCIAL WORKERS (1960), *Morals and the Social Worker*, A Report of the 1959 Conference.

ATKINSON, J. (1968), 'On the sociology of suicide', *Sociological Review*, *16*, 83-92.

ATTLEE, C. (1920), *The Social Worker*, London: Bell.

AUSTIN, L. N. (1950), 'Supervision of the experienced caseworker' in KASIUS (ed.) (1950).

BARRETT, S. J. (1966), 'Psychiatric record keeping in the military', *Am. J. Psychiatry*, *120*, 887.

BARTLETT, E. (1958), 'Social factors in recall', pp. 47-54 in MACCOBY, E. E., NEWCOMB, T. M. & HARTLEY, E. L.

BARTLETT, F. (ed.) (1939), *The Study of Society*, London: Kegan Paul.

BARTLETT, HARRIET (1961), *Social Work Practice in the Health Field*, New York: National Association of Social Workers.

BARTLETT, HARRIET (1965), 'Social work practice' in *Encyclopaedia of Social Work*.

BATTEN, T. R. (1967), *The Non-Directive Approach in Group and Community Work*, London: OUP.

BECK, I. F. (1948), 'Essay in medical social record keeping', *Social Work* (UK), *5*, 2, 151-8.

BINGHAM, W. V. D. & BRUCE, V. M. (1931), *How to Interview*, New York: Harper & Row.

BLUM, RICHARD H. & EZEKIEL, JONATHAN (1962), *Clinical*

Records for Mental Health Services, Springfield Ill.: Charles C. Thomas.

BOEHM, W. W. (1959), *The Social Casework Method in Social Work Education*, New York: Council on Social Work Education.

BORGATTA, E. F., FANSHIEL, D. & MEYER, H. J. (1960), *Social Workers' Perceptions of Clients*, New York: Russell Sage Foundation.

BORK, KATHRYN (1953), 'A staff examination of recording skill: Part I', *Child Welfare*, 32, 2, 3-8.

BORK, KATHRYN (1953), 'A Staff examination of recording skill: Part II', *Child Welfare*, 32, 3, 11-14.

BRISTOL, MARGARET (1936), *Handbook on Social Case Recording* (Social Service Monographs 36), University of Chicago Press.

BRITISH ASSOCIATION OF SOCIAL WORKERS (1970), *Research and Social Work*, Monograph no. 4.

BRITISH ASSOCIATION OF SOCIAL WORKERS (1971), *Discussion Paper No. 1: Confidentiality in Social Work*.

BRITISH HOSPITAL JOURNAL (1970), 'Medical records', August 1681.

BRODY, E. B. (1967), 'Recording cross-culturally useful psychiatric interview data', *Am. J. Psychiatry*, *123*, 446.

BRODY, E. B., NEWMAN, R. & REDLICH, F. C. (1951), 'Sound recording and the problem of evidence in psychiatry', *Science*, *113*, 379-80.

BROWN, MALCOLM (1970), 'An analysis of probation service practice', unpublished Ph.D. thesis, University of Bradford.

BROWN, S. C. (1939), 'The methods of social caseworkers in BARTLETT, F. (ed.).

BROWN, S. C. & GLOYNE, E. R. (1966), *The Field Training of Social Workers*, London: Allen & Unwin.

BRUNER, JEROME S. (1958), 'Social psychology and perception', in MACCOBY, E. E., NEWCOMB, T. M. & HARTLEY, E. L.

BRUNO, FRANK J. (1928), 'Some casework recording limitations of verbatim recording', *Social Forces*, 6, 4, 532-8.

BUREAU OF PUBLIC ASSISTANCE SOCIAL SECURITY ADMINISTRATION (1947), *Case Records in Public Assistance*, Federal Security Agency, Technical Training Service, *1*.

BURGESS, ERNEST W. (1928), 'What social case records should contain to be useful for sociological interpretation', *Social Forces, 6,* 4, 524-32.

BURNETT, A. E. & HOLLAND, W. W. (1968), 'The medical record and the computer' in MCLACHLAN, G. & SHEGOG, R. A.

BURTON, D. & BARSTOW, D. W. (1970), 'Use of evaluation in staff development', *Social Work Today, 1,* 8, 41.

BUTRYM, ZOFIA (1968), *Medical Social Work in Action,* London: Bell.

CAMERON, E. S. (1970), Letter to editor, *Medical Social Work,* 22, 27.

CAREY, H. E. (1970), Letter to editor, *Medical Social Work,* 22, 288.

CARTER, G. (1958), 'Social work: Community organisation methods', p. 201 in FRIEDLANDER, W.

CARTER, G. (1959), 'The nature of Judgement Data' in *Use of Judgements as Data,* New York: NASW.

CHARITY ORGANISATION QUARTERLY (1926), *Fifty Years Ago,* no. 18.

CHILDREY, RACHEL (1933), 'Case recording: A committee report', *Family, 13,* 299-301.

CITY GUILD OF HELP (1903), Unpublished Minute Book, Bradford.

CLIFFORD, W. (1961), 'Specialisation and integration in social work', *Case Conference,* 8, 3, 30.

COHEN, NATHAN E. (1958), *Social Work in the American Tradition,* New York: Dryden Press.

COLLINS, JOAN (1965a), *Social Casework in a General Medical Practice,* London: Pitman.

COLLINS, JOAN (1965b), 'The guinea pig', *Case Conference, 11,* 7, 229.

COLLINS, JOAN (1967), *A New Look at Social Work,* London: Pitman.

COPE, C. B. (1968), 'Record linkage in medicine' in ACHESON, E. D.

COURTENY, MICHAEL (1968), *Sexual Discord in Marriage,* London: Tavistock Publications.

COVNER, BERNARD J. (1944), 'Studies in phonographic recordings of verbal material', *J. General Psychology, 30,* 181-203.

CROFTON, MORGAN W. (1870), 'On the proof of the law of errors of observations', *Philosophical Transactions of the Royal Society*, *160*, 175-87.

CROSS, K. W., DROAR, J. & ROBERTS, J. L. (1968), 'Electronic processing of hospital records' in MCLACHLAN, G. & SHEGOG, R. A.

DALE, T. W. & ROBERTS, J. L. (1968a), 'Errors in a hospital record system' in MCLACHLAN, G. & SHEGOG, R. A.

DALE, T. W. & ROBERTS, J. L. (1968b), 'The identification of patients and their records in a hospital' in MCLACHLAN, G. & SHEGOG, R. A.

DAVIS, M. (1964), 'Interviewing techniques', *New Society*, *3*, 90, 13.

DAVISON, EVELYN H. (1965), *Social Casework*, London: Baillière Tindall & Cox.

DINWOODIE, H. P. (1970), 'Simple computer facilities in general practice', *J. Royal College of General Practitioners*, *19*, 94, 269-81.

DODV, S. R. A. (1969), 'Requirements of medical records—the clinician's point of view', *WHO/HSNat. Com.*, *70*, 259.

DOLLARD, J. (1935), *Criteria for the Life History*, New Haven: Yale University Press.

DUDLEY, H. A. F. (1971), 'Clinical method', *Lancet*, *i*, 7688, 35-7.

DUMAS, N. S. (ed.) (1968), 'Research utilization and dissemination', proceedings of a regional conference sponsored by the Social and Rehabilitation Service, Department of Health, Education and Welfare, Washington and the Regional Rehabilitation Research Institute, University of Florida.

DWYER, M. & URBANOWSKI, M. (1965), 'Student process recording: A plea for structure', *Social Casework*, *46*, 5, 283.

EDWARDS, F. (1969), 'Some thoughts on performance assessment', *Case Conference*, *16*, 8, 319.

ELDRED, S., *et al.* (1954), 'A procedure for the systematic analysis of psychotherapeutic interviews', *Psychiatry*, *17*, 4.

ELIOT, THOMAS D. (1928), 'Objectivity and subjectivity in the case record', *Social Forces*, 6, 4, 539-44.

ENCYCLOPAEDIA OF SOCIAL WORK (1965), New York: NASW.

ESSLINGER, E. (1949), *The Social Case Record as an Instrument of Social Research*, Cape Town: Juta.

ETZIONI, AMITAI (ed.) (1969), *The Semi-Professions and their Organisation*, New York: The Free Press.

FAMILY SERVICE ASSOCIATION OF AMERICA (1943), *The Use of Confidential Case Record Information*, Committee on Confidential Nature of Casework Information, New York.

FARRAR, C. B. (1906), 'The making of psychiatric records', *Am. J. Insanity*, 62, 479-509.

FELDMAN, YONATA (1957), 'Students' training needs as reflected in their recorded material', *Smith College Studies in Social Work*, 27, 2.

FENLASON, A. F. (1962), *Essentials in Interviewing*, New York: Harper & Row.

FENTON, N. & WILTSE, K. (1963), *Group Methods in the Public Welfare Program*, Palo Alto: Pacific Books.

FIBUSH, E. & REEVE, M. (1959), 'Some current contradictions in the field of Casework', *Social Casework*, 40, 18.

FINESTONE, S. (1962), 'The scientific component in the casework field curriculum' in KASIUS, C.

FIRTH, CATHERINE M. (1970), 'Confidentiality of personal information supplied to public authorities', *G.L.C. Quarterly Bulletin of the Research and Intelligence Unit*, no. 10, 5-11.

FORDER, ANTHONY (1966), *Social Casework and Administration*, London: Faber.

FOREN, R. J. W. (1969), 'An investigation into the origins and development of social casework in prisons', unpublished M.A. Thesis, University of Bradford.

FORMAN, F. & FAIRBAIRN, ELSPETH (1968), *Social Casework in General Practice*, London: OUP.

FRENCH, D. G. (1952), *Measuring Results in Social Work*, New York: Columbia University Press.

FRIEDLANDER, W. (ed.) (1958), *Concepts and Methods of Social Work*, New York: Prentice-Hall.

FRINGS, J. (1957), 'Experimental system of recording', *Social Casework*, 38, 55.

FROELICH, C. P. (1958), 'The completeness and accuracy of counselling interview reports', *J. General Psychology*, 58, 81-96.

GAY, E. (1958), 'Collecting data by case recording', *Social Work*, 3, 76.

GLAGEBROOK, P. R. (1968), 'Medical confidences, research and the law', in ACHESON, E. D. (ed.).

GOETSCHIUS, GEORGE W. (1969), *Working with Community Groups*, London: Routledge & Kegan Paul.

GOFFMAN, ERVING (1961), 'The moral career of the mental patient', in *Asylums*, New York: Doubleday, Anchor Books.

HAINES, J. (1966), 'Evaluation as a part of supervision', *Case Conference*, 13, 5, 179.

HAMILTON, GORDON (1946), *Principles of Social Case Recording*, New York: Columbia University Press.

HAMILTON, GORDON (1951), *Theory and Practice of Social Casework*, New York: Columbia University Press.

HAWKER, A. (1971), 'Computer privacy', *Social Work Today*, 2, 10.

HENDRICKS, THOMASINE (1957), *Social Work Performance, Standards and Evaluation*, Washington: Department of Health, Welfare and Education.

HERBST, P. G. (1962), *Autonomous Group Functioning*, London: Tavistock Publications.

HERBST, P. G. (1970), *Behavioural Worlds*, London: Tavistock Publications.

HERTZOG, ELIZABETH (1959), *Some Guide Lines for Evaluative Research*, Washington: Department of Health, Education and Welfare, Social Security Administration, Children's Bureau.

HERZOG, HERTA (1948), *Training Guide on the Technique of Qualitative Interviews*, Universitetets Studentkontor, Oslo.

HEYWOOD, JEAN (1964), *An Introduction to Teaching Casework Skills*, London: Routledge & Kegan Paul.

HOCHWALD, HILDE LANGENBERGER (1952), 'The use of case records in research', *Social Casework*, 33, 2, 71-6.

HODES, C. (1968), 'The structure and function of a file of patient health data in general practice', *J. Royal College of General Practitioners*, *15*, 4, 286-91.

HOEFNAGELS, G. P. (1957), *Reporting in Cases of Juvenile Civil Law* (English summary), Van Gorcum.

HOLDER, VERONICA (1962), 'Our present discontents', *Case Conference*, 8, 9, 231.

HOLLIS, FLORENCE (1964), *Casework*, New York: Random House.

HOLLIS, FLORENCE (1967), 'The coding and application of a typology of casework treatment', *Social Casework*, *48*, 489.

HOLLIS, FLORENCE (1968), *A Typology of Casework Treatment*, New York: FSAA.

HOME OFFICE (PROBATION DIVISION) (1953), *Notes on the Records of Supervision for Use by Probation Officers in Accordance with Rule 47 of the Probation Rules 1949*, HMSO.

HOME OFFICE (1962), *Report of the Department Committee on the Probation Service* (Morrison Report), HMSO.

HOME OFFICE (1963), *Advisory Council on Organisation of After-Care*, HMSO.

HOWARD, LUANA (1969), 'Social work recording in medical notes', *Medical Social Work*, *21*, 10, 299-307.

HUNT, ARTHUR (1959), *Casework Recording II*, HH 51/46/61, Home Office, HMSO.

HUNT, J., BLENKNER, M. & KOGAN, L. S. (1950), *Testing Results in Social Casework*, New York: FSAA.

HUNT, J. & KOGAN, L. S. (1950), *Measuring Results in Social Casework*, New York: FSAA.

HURWITZ, J. I. (1956), 'Systematizing social group work practice', *Social Work*, *1*, 63.

HYMAN, H. H., HART, C. W., COBB, W. J., FELDMAN, J. J. & STEMBER, C. H. (1954), *Interviewing in Social Research*, Chicago University Press.

INNES, G. & WEIR, R. D. (1968), 'Patient identification on a regional basis in MCLACHLAN, G. & SHEGOG, R. A.

INSTITUTE OF ALMONERS (1956), Memorandum of the Records Committee, *Almoner*, *1*, 3, 56 and 2, 16.

ITZIN, FRANK (1960), 'The use of tape recording in field work', *Social Casework*, *41*, 197-202.

JACOB, K. K. (1965, 2nd edn), *Methods and Fields of Social Work in India*, London: Asia Publishing House.

JACOBS, G. (1968), 'The reification of the notion of sub-culture in public welfare', *Social Casework*, *49*, 527-34.

JAMESON, M. J. (1968), 'A system of recording the family history in general practice', *J. Royal College of General Practitioners*, *16*, 2, 135-143.

JARVIS, F. V. (1969), *Probation Officers' Manual*, London: Butterworth.

JEFFREYS, MARGOT (1965), *An Anatomy of Social Welfare Services*, London: Michael Joseph.

JOEL, W. & SHAPIRO, D. (1968), 'Some principles and procedures for group psychotherapy' in MURO & FREEMAN.

KADUSHIN, A. (1956), 'Interview observations as a teaching device', *Social Casework*, *37*, 334, 341.

KADUSHIN, A. & SCHENK, Q. (1962), 'An experiment in teaching an integrated methods course' in KASIUS, C. (1962).

KASIUS, CORA (ed.) (1950), *Principles and Techniques in Social Casework—Selected Articles*, New York: FSAA.

KASIUS, CORA (ed.) (1962), *Social Casework in the Fifties—Selected Articles*, New York: FSAA.

KASTELL, JEAN (1962), *Casework in Child Care*, London: Routledge & Kegan Paul.

KELLEY, MINNIE E. (1962), 'Additional uses of tape recordings in social work education', *Social Casework*, *43*, 1, 26-9.

KENT, BESSIE (1969), *Social Work Supervision in Practice*, Oxford: Pergamon.

KITSUSE, J. I. & CICOUREL, A. Y. (1968), 'A note on the uses of official statistics', *Social Problems*, *11*, 2, 131-9.

KNIGHT, J. F. (1965), Correspondence, *Almoner*, *17*, 8, 260.

KOGAN, L. S. (1950), 'The electrical recording of social casework interviews', *Social Casework*, *31*, 371-8.

KOGAN, L. S. & BROWN, B. H. (1954), 'A two year study of case record uses', *Social Casework*, *35*, 6, 252-57.

KOGAN, L. S., HUNT, J. MCV. & BARTELME, PHYLLIS (1953), *A Follow-up Study of the Results of Social Casework*, New York: FSSA.

KONOPKA, GISELA (1954), *Group Work in the Institution*, New York: Association Press.

KONOPKA, GISELA (1963), *Social Group Work—A Helping Process*, Englewood Cliffs: Prentice-Hall.

KUBIE, L. S. (1947) (Member of Round Table on), 'Problems in clinical research', *Am. J. Orthopsy, 17*, 196-203.

LADEN, H. N. & GILDERSLEEVE, T. R. (1963), *System Design for Computer Applications*, New York: John Wiley.

LANCET (1967), Editorial comment, *i*, 399: (1968) editorial comment, *ii*, 396; KENNEDY, F., *et al.*, *ii*, 1230-3.

LAWRANCE, K. L. (1912), 'The importance of good casework', *Charity Organisation Review*, March.

LEE, PORTER R. (1932), Foreword in SAYLES, M. G.

LEEVES, R. E. (1965), 'The probation officer's use of time', *Case Conference, 12*, 2, 44-5.

LEHRMAN, L. J. (1962), 'The integration of class and field in professional education', in KASIUS, C. (1962).

LEVINE, JEROME M. & MURPHY, GARDNER (1958), 'The learning and forgetting of controversial material' in MACCOBY, E. E., NEWCOMB, T. M. & HARTLEY, E. L.

LEWIN, KURT (1958), 'Group decision and social change' in MACCOBY, E. E., NEWCOMB, T. M. & HARTLEY, E. L.

LEWIS, CAROL A. (1969), 'Research in the field of routine hospital record techniques', *WHO/HS/Nat. Com.*, 70, 256.

LITTLE, KENNETH B. & SHNEIDMAN, EDWIN S. (1959), 'Congruencies among interpretations of psychological test and anamnestic data', *Psychological Monographs General and Applied, 73*, 6, no. 476.

LITTLE, RUBY (1949), 'Diagnostic recording', *Social Casework, 30*, 1, 15-19.

LUNDBERG, GEORGE A. (1926), 'Casework and the statistical method', *J. of Social Forces, 5*, 1, 61-5.

MAAS, HENRY (1966), *Five Fields of Social Service*, New York: NASW.

MCCAFFERY, M. (1962), 'Criteria for student progress in fieldwork' in KASIUS, C.

MACCOBY, E. E., NEWCOMB, T. & HARTLEY, E. (eds) (1958), *Readings in Social Psychology*, London: Methuen.

MACDONALD, M. E. (1959), 'Compatability of theory and

method' in *NASW, Use of Judgements as Data in Social Work Research*.

MACIVER, ALSAGER (1935), 'An old case box', *Charity Organisation Quarterly*, 9, April, 55-60.

MCLACHLAN, G. (ed.) (1964), *Problems and Progress in Medical Care*, London: OUP.

MCLACHLAN, G. & SHEGOG, R. A. (eds) (1968), *Computers in the Service of Medicine*, I and II, London: OUP.

MACLENNAN, BERYCE W. & FELSENFELD, NAOMI (1968), *Group Counselling and Psychotherapy with Adolescents*, New York: Columbia University Press.

MADGE, JOHN (1953), *The Tools of Social Science*, London: Longmans.

MATTINSON, J. (1970), *Marriage and Mental Handicap*, London: Duckworth.

MERRIFIELD, A. R., FASSLER, L., LANE, H. J. & LOCKHART, H. (1960), 'A new recording system for medical settings', *Social Casework, 41, 5,* 254-7.

MERTON, R., FISKE, M. & KENDALL, P. (1956), *The Focused Interview*, New York: The Free Press.

MILES, ARTHUR P. (1965), 'The utility of case records in probation and parole', *J. Criminal Law, Criminology and Police Science, 56,* 3, 285-93.

MILLER, IRVING (1960), 'Supervision in group work', *Social Work, 5,* 1, 69-76.

MINISTRY OF HEALTH (1964), *The Standardization of Hospital Medical Records* (Tunbridge Report), HMSO.

MINISTRY OF HEALTH (1970), *Handicapped Children in Care of Local Authorities and Voluntary Organisations*, HMSO.

MINISTRY OF HOUSING AND LOCAL GOVERNMENT (1968), *Report of the Committee on Local Authority and Allied Personal Social Services* (Chairman: F. Seebohm), HMSO.

MITCHELL, J. H. (1969), *A New Look at Hospital Case Records*, London: H. K. Lewis.

MOORE, ELON H. (1933-4), 'How accurate are case records?' *Social Forces, 12,* 4, 498-507.

MOURIN, K. A. (1970), 'Forms and reforms', *J. Royal College of General Practitioners, 19*, 91, 114-20.

MOWAT, CHARLES LOCH (1961), *Charity Organisation Society 1869-1913*, London: Methuen.

MUNRO, ALISTAIR & MCCULLOCH, WALLACE (1969), *Psychiatry for Social Workers*, Oxford: Pergamon.

MUNRO, MARGUERITE (1951), 'Modern casework recording', *Social Work Journal*, October, 184-7 and 197.

MURCH, M. (1971), 'Privacy—no concern of social work', *Social Work Today, 2, 5*, 6-8.

MURO, J. J. & FREEMAN, S. L. (eds) (1968), *Readings in Group Counselling*, Scranton, Penn.: International Textbook Co.

NATIONAL ASSOCIATION OF PROBATION OFFICERS (1968), 'Case recording in Probation and after-care', *Probation Papers no. 5*.

NATIONAL ASSOCIATION OF SOCIAL WORKERS (1959), *Use of Judgements as Data in Social Work Research*, New York: NASW.

NATIONAL CONFERENCE OF SOCIAL WELFARE (1969), 'Social work practice', New York: Columbia University Press.

NATIONAL CONFERENCE OF SOCIAL WORK (1944), *Proceedings*, New York: Columbia University Press.

NEVILLE, E. (1914), 'Organisation', *Charity Organisation Review, 35*, 125-30.

NEW SOCIETY (1963), 'Social work training doubts', 2, 49, 16; Correspondence (EILEEN YOUNGHUSBAND), 'Social work training', 2, 51, 27-8; Notes—Social Work Casebook Research, 2, 64, 19.

NICHOLDS, E. (1966), *In-Service Casework Training*, New York: Columbia University Press.

NICHOLLS, G. K. (1966), 'The science and art of the casework relationship', *Smith College Studies in Social Work, 36*, 2, 109-26.

NOBLE, J. (1971), 'Protecting the public's privacy in computerized health and welfare information systems', *Social Work* (USA), 16, 1, 35-41.

O'CONNELL, B. & MCFARLANE, A. H. (1970), 'A medical care information system', *Medical Care*, 8, 1.

OPIT, L. J. & WOODROFFE, F. J. (1970), 'Computer-held clinical record system—I Description of system', *BMJ*, 4, October, 76-79.

PANNOR, REUBEN & PETERSON, MARION V. (1936), 'Current trends in case recording', *Child Welfare*, 42, 5, 230-4.

PARAD, H. J. & CAPLAN, GERALD (1960), 'Studying families in crisis', *Social Work*, 5, 5, 3-15.

PARKER, R. (1966), *Decision in Child Care*, London: Allen & Unwin.

PARKER, R. (1971), *Planning for Deprived Children*, London: National Children's Homes.

PERLMAN, HELEN HARRIS (1957), *Social Casework*, New York: Columbia University Press.

PHELPS, HAROLD A. (1927), 'The case record and scientific method', *Family*, 8, 4, 103-9.

POLANSKY, NORMAN A. (ed.) (1960), *Social Work Research*, Chicago University Press.

PRESTON, M. G., MUDD, E. H. & FROSCHER, H. B. (1953), 'Factors affecting movement in casework', *Social Casework*, 34, 3, 103-11.

PRESTON, M. G., MUDD, E. H., PELTZ, WILLIAM L. & FROSCHER, HAZEL B. (1950), 'An experimental study of a method of abstracting the content of social case records', *J. of Abnormal and Social Psychology*, 45, 628-46.

PRICE, L. G. (1951), 'The keeping of records for statistical and analytical purposes', *Almoner*, 3, 9, 315-21 and 363-72.

PUMPHREY, M. W. (1959), *The Teaching of Values and Ethics in Social Work Education*, Social Work Curriculum Study XIII, New York: Council on Social Work Education.

RAPOPORT, L. (ed.) (1963), *Consultation in Social Work Practice*, New York: NASW.

RAWLEY, CALLMAN (1939), 'A functional examination of recording', *Family*, 19, 298-305.

REDL, FRITZ & WINEMAN, DAVID (1951), *Children Who Hate*, Chicago: The Free Press.

REDLICH, FREDERICK C., DOLLARD, JOHN & NEWMAN, RICHARD (1950), 'High fidelity recording of psychotherapeutic interviews', *Am. J. Psychiatry*, 107, 42-8.

REEVE, G. H. (1934), 'Demonstration as a method of education in training for Psychiatric social work', *Am. J. Orthopsy*, 4, 3, 359-64.

REEVE, G. H. (1939), 'Trends in Therapy', *Am. J. Orthopsy*, 9, 4, 743-7.

RENNISON, G. A. (1962), *Man on his Own: Social Work and Industrial Society*, Melbourne University Press.

RESNICK, R. B. & BALTER, H. G. (1934), 'Withholding information from law enforcement bodies', *Social Service Review*, 8, 4, 668-77.

RICHARDSON, S. A. (1965), *Interviewing*, New York: Basic Books.

RICHMOND, MARY (1917), *Social Diagnosis*, New York: Russell Sage Foundation

RICHMOND, MARY (1925), 'Why case records?', *Family*, 6, 214-16.

RIPPLE, LILIAN (1964), *Motivation, Capacity and Opportunity*, Social Service Monographs, 2nd Series, Chicago: University of Chicago Press.

ROBINSON, G. A. (1966), *Hospital Administration*, London: Butterworth.

ROBINSON, JAMES T. & COHEN, LOUIS D. (1954), 'Individual bias in psychology reports', *J. Clinical Psychology*, 10, 333-6.

ROBINSON, VIRGINIA P. (1921), 'Analysis of processes in the records of family case working agencies', *Family*, 2, 5, 101-6.

ROBINSON, VIRGINIA P. (1930), *A Changing Psychology in Social Casework*, Chapel Hill: University of North Carolina Press.

ROBINSON, VIRGINIA P. (1949), *The Dynamics of Supervision under Functional Controls*, Philadelphia: University of Pennsylvania Press.

RÓSE, G. (1957), 'Assessing the results of social work', *Sociological Review*, 5, 225-37.

ROSENBLATT, A. & MAYER, J. (1970), 'Reduction of uncertainty in child placement decisions', *Social Work*, 15, 52-61.

RUTTER, MICHAEL & GRAHAM, PHILIP (1968), 'The reliability and validity of the psychiatric assessment of the child', *British J. Psychiatry, 114, 510, 563-92.*

SACKHEIM, GERTRUDE (1949), 'Suggestions on recording techniques', *Social Casework, 30, 1, 20-5.*

SASSIN, E. & DALTON, MICHAEL H. (1960), 'Recognition of organic factors in behaviour disorders', *Social Work, 5, 3, 36-9.*

SAYLES, M. G. (ed.) (1932), *Child Guidance Cases,* New York: The Commonwealth Fund.

SCHRAEGER, J. (1955), 'Child care staff recording', *Social Casework, 36, 2, 74-81.*

SCHREIBER, PAUL (1956), 'Statistics', in ENCYCLOPAEDIA OF SOCIAL WORK.

SCHWEINITZ, E. de & SCHWEINITZ, KARL de (1962), *Interviewing in the Social Services,* London: National Council of Social Service.

SCOTT, RICHARD W. (1969), 'Professional employees in a bureaucratic structure' in ETZIONI, A. (ed.).

SELLER, SHELDON & TAYLOR, JOY (1965), 'The malevolent transformation', *Social Work, 10, 3, 82-91.*

SERVICE, PAMELA (1969), 'The use of intake systems in hospitals', *Medical Social Work, 21, 10, 308-13.*

SHEFFIELD, ADA ELIOT (1920), *The Social Case History,* New York: Russell Sage Foundation.

SHYNE, ANN (1960), 'Social work research: Use of available material' in POLANSKY, N. (ed.).

SHYNE, ANN (1965), 'Social work research' in ENCYCLOPAEDIA OF SOCIAL WORK.

SIMPSON, J., ARSDOL, M., & SABAGH, G. (1965), 'Records matching as a technique for social research', *Sociology and Social Research, 50, 1, 89-100.*

SMITH, JAMES OTIS, SJOBERG, GIDEON & PHILLIPS, VIRGINIA (1969), 'The use and meaning of psychiatric records', *International J. Social Psychiatry, 15, 2, 129-35.*

SMITH, R. *et al.* (1966), 'The Woolwich and Erith Project', *Lancet, i, 650-4.*

SNELLING, J. (1947), 'Some notes on hospital interviewing', *Social Work* (UK), January.

SPEIRS, R. W. (1959), *Casework Recording I*, P.B.N. 89/6/32, Home Office.

STOCKBRIDGE, M. E. (1968), 'Social case recording', *Case Conference*, *15*, 8, 307-12.

STONE, SARAH & KERSCHNER, EDITH N. (1959), 'Creative recording', *Child Welfare*, *38*, 1, 1-8.

STROUP, HERBERT HEWITT (1948), *Social Work—An Introduction to the Field*, New York: American Book Co.

STUBBLEFIELD, R. L. & CAMP, B. W. (1959), 'Use of Keysort system in maintaining clinic records for research', *Am. J. Orthopsy*, 29, 827-8.

SWIFT, LYNTON B. (1928), 'Can the sociologist and social worker agree on the content of case records?', *Social Forces*, 6, 4, 535-8.

SYTZ, FLORENCE (1949), 'Teaching recording', *J. Social Casework 30*, 10, 399-405.

TAYLOR, ALICE L. (1953), 'Case recording: An administrative responsibility', *Social Casework*, 34, 6, 240-6.

TAYLOR, T. R. (1969), 'The medical social worker in the medical clinic', *Medical Social Work*, 22, 6, 200-7.

TENNANT, GERTRUDE (1927), 'Prize medical social case record', *Social Service Review*, *1*, 3, 443-469.

THORNTON, DORIS (1963), 'Communication in writing as part of social casework', *Almoner*, *15*, 10, 291-6.

TIMMS, NOEL W. (1961), 'Social work in action—A historical study (I)', *Case Conference*, 7, 10, 259-63.

TIMMS, NOEL W. (1964a), 'The psychiatric social worker', *Case Conference*, *10*, 8, 246-9.

TIMMS, NOEL W. (1964b), *Social Casework*, London: Routledge & Kegan Paul.

TODD, F. J. (1956), 'Psychiatric social work in a mental deficiency hospital', *British J. Psychiatric Social Work*, 3, 4, 25-7.

TOREN, NINA (1969), 'Semi-professionalism and social work —A theoretical perspective', in ETZIONI, A. (ed.).

TOWLE, CHARLOTTE (1941), *Social Case Records from Psychiatric Clinics*, Chicago: University of Chicago Press.

ULLMANN, ALICE & KASSERBAUM, GENE G. (1961), 'Referrals and services in a medical social work department', *Social Service Review*, 65, 258-67.

UNITED NATIONS (TECHNICAL ASSISTANCE OFFICE IN EUROPE)
(1959), *Social Case Records for Teaching Purposes*.

VASEY, I. (1968), 'Developing a data storage and retrieval
system', *Social Casework*, 49, 7, 414-17.

WALLIN, F. W., Preface in FRENCH, D. G.

WARNER, MALCOLM & STONE, MICHAEL (1970), *The Data
Bank Society*, London: Allen & Unwin.

WASSER, E. (1957), 'The caseworker as research interviewer
in follow-up studies', *Social Casework*, 38, 8, 423-30.

WHEELER, STANTON (ed.) (1969), *On Record*, New York:
Russell Sage Foundation.

WHITEBROOK, O. E. (1945), 'The professional confidence in
the casework relationship', *Family*, 26, 7, 250-7.

WILES, PAUL (1971), 'Criminal statistics and sociological ex-
planations of crime', 174-90, in *Crime and Delinquency
in Britain*, CARSON, W. G. & WILES, PAUL (eds.), London:
Martin Robertson.

WILKIE, CHARLOTTE H. (1963), 'A study of distortions in
recording interviews', *Social Work*, 8, 3, 31-6.

WILKINS, L. T. (1964), *Social Deviance*, London: Tavistock
Publications.

WILKINS, L. T. (1967), *Social Policy Action and Research*,
London: Social Science Paperbacks.

WILKINS, L. T. & CHANDLER, ANN (1965), 'Confidence and
competence in decision making', *British J. Criminology*,
5, 1, 22-35.

WILMER, H. A. (1968), 'Television as participant recorder',
Am. J. Psychiatry, 124, 9, 1157-63.

WILSON, A. T. M. (1955), 'A note on the social sanctions of
social research', *Sociological Review*, 3, 109-16.

WILSON, G. & RYLAND, G. (1949), *Social Group Work Practice*, Boston: Houghton Mifflin.

WITTENBERG, RUDOLPH M. (1947), *So You Want to Help
People?*, New York: Association Press.

WITTS, L. J. (1968), 'People in confidence: The expanding
circle', in ACHESON, E. D. (ed.).

WORKING DEFINITION OF SOCIAL WORK PRACTICE (1965), in
ENCYCLOPAEDIA OF SOCIAL WORK.

WORLD HEALTH ORGANISATION (1969), Hospital Medical

Records. *W.H.O./H.S./Nat. Com. 70*, nos. 252-9, Editorial comments

WRIGHT, HERBERT F. (1967), *Recording and Analyzing Child Behavior*, New York: Harper & Row.

YOUNG, ERLE F. (1925), 'The scientific study of social case records', *J. Applied Sociology*, 9, 4, 283-9.

YOUNGHUSBAND, EILEEN (1949), *Report on Employment and Training of Social Workers*, Edinburgh: Constable for Carnegie Foundation.

YOUNGHUSBAND, EILEEN (chairman) (1959), *Report of the Working Party on Social Workers in the Local Authority Health and Welfare Services*, HMSO.

YOUNGHUSBAND, EILEEN (ed.) (1966), *New Developments in Casework*, London: Allen & Unwin.

YOUNGHUSBAND, EILEEN (1968), 'The nature of social work', in LOCKHEAD, A.V.S. (ed.), *A Reader in Social Administration*, London: Constable.

ZUCKER, E. M. M. (1964), 'Records and Statistics', *Almoner*, 17, 5, 133-40.

Printed and bound by CPI Group (UK) Ltd, Croydon, CR0 4YY

21/10/2024

01777086-0001